IN CHRIST & ON TRACK

The Essential Paul

Morris A. Inch

University Press of America,® Inc.
Lanham · Boulder · New York · Toronto · Plymouth, UK

Copyright © 2008 by
University Press of America,® Inc.
4501 Forbes Boulevard
Suite 200
Lanham, Maryland 20706
UPA Acquisitions Department (301) 459-3366

Estover Road
Plymouth PL6 7PY
United Kingdom

All rights reserved
Printed in the United States of America
British Library Cataloging in Publication Information Available

Library of Congress Control Number: 2007940279
ISBN-13: 978-0-7618-3965-1 (paperback : alk. paper)
ISBN-10: 0-7618-3965-8 (paperback : alk. paper)

∞™ The paper used in this publication meets the minimum
requirements of American National Standard for Information
Sciences—Permanence of Paper for Printed Library Materials,
ANSI Z39.48—1984

CONTENTS

Preface	v
Acknowledgment	vii
Correspondence	1
Jesus of History	13
Christ of Faith	25
One Among Many	33
A Corporate Identity	41
In Situ	49
Salvation History	57
The Angels' View	65
Paul As Paradigm	71
Exhortations	79
Endnotes	87
Bibliography	91
Index	93

PREFACE

The expression *in Christ* epitomizes Paul's teaching as none other. It or its equivalent is said to occur 165 times in his correspondence. Even so, the topic characteristically receives only summary treatment. Consequently, I propose a more extended discussion, one that also explores select related matters—all of which may be said to focus on *the essential Paul*.

Initially, an inductive approach will best serve our purposes. This will touch on the Pauline correspondence in representative fashion, thereby illustrating some of the rich nuances associated with this provocative allusion.

After that, we explore the first of three dualities. It consists of the Jesus of history as set over against the Christ of faith. Then, in turn, it anticipates the massive literature associated with the quest for the historical Jesus.

The second duality explores the personal and corporate settings of being in Christ. The former since the Christian life cannot be lived by proxy. The latter because in coming to Christ one encounters community.

A third duality considers the physical setting of Paul's ministry, along with its location in salvation history. This serves to remind us that life evolves in a space/time continuum, thereby revealing its continuing relevance.

The final segment looks at the topic from three distinctive perspectives. First, in the light of Jesus' ascension. Subsequently, Paul as a prime exemplar of the Christian faith—viewed from the purview of the early church fathers. After that, considering some of the apostle's apt exhortations.

In order to prime the pump, consider a case in point. "Therefore," Paul enthusiastically reasons, "if anyone is in Christ, he is a new creation; the old has gone, the new has come! All this is from God, who reconciled us to himself through Christ and gave us the ministry of reconciliation" (2 Cor. 5:17-18). *The old has gone* is an aorist tense indicating an action now completed, and *the new has come* is a perfect tense suggesting a past action with continuing effects.

As for extended commentary:

The two sentences together emphasize the eschatological centrality of Christ. "In

Christ" the old ends and the new—a new creation—begins. . . . The crucified and risen Christ is the divine agent of universal salvation, the divider of history into aeons, that 'no longer' aeon when all things were "old" and the "now" aeon when all things have become, and are, "new."[1]

All this is God's doing, as the divine benefactor. Christ serves as the redemptive agent. As a result, believers have been entrusted with the urgent ministry of reconciliation. This, however, is simply to note the proverbial tip of the iceberg. Much more awaits our attention.

Morris A. Inch
Russellville, AR
September, 2007

ACKNOWLEDGMENT

A special word of appreciation is due my beloved wife Joan, not only for her editing and formatting of the test, but her loving encouragement over the years.

CORRESPONDENCE

An inductive approach serves best at the outset, rather than to fall into the temptation of dealing with broad generalities. In particular, I will touch on a number of representative texts drawn from the Pauline correspondence. More expressly, allowing for the traditional classifications: early, general, prison, and pastoral epistles.

Early Epistles

Galatians first invites our attention. Controversy surrounds the occasion on which the epistle was composed. According to one theory, it was written during Paul's first missionary journey and before the Jerusalem Council (cf. Acts 15). If not, then shortly thereafter.

The letter addresses a serious problem that had arisen in Galatia, variously understood as an ethnic or political designation.

> That it was a serious problem, we can tell from the abruptness with which Paul introduced the matter, without his usual opening section of tactful commendation of the local church. The problem seems to have been some new line of teaching, probably introduced soon after Paul's departure (1:6), by an unnamed person (1:9) or persons (1:7).[1]

In any case, Paul signifies that it amounts to a distortion of the true gospel (cf. 1:7), expressly in that it requires circumcision in order to be saved (cf. 5:2).

It may be significant that the apostle's first use of *in Christ* occurs in a corporate setting. He pointedly observes, "I was personally unknown to the churches of Judea that are in Christ" (1:22). While they had likely heard of his disruptive activities, they had no personal acquaintance with him.

This is also a subtle reminder that there were churches scattered elsewhere. Such as would give expression to a variety of cultural preferences. Then, in turn, as an evidence that God delights in constructive diversity—as over against a drab uniformity.

The polemic builds.

> We who are Jews by birth and not 'Gentile sinners' know that a man is not justified by observing the law, but by faith in Jesus Christ. So we, too, have put our faith in Christ Jesus that we may be justified by faith in Christ and not by observing the law, because by observing the law no one will be justified (2:15-16).

Three times the apostle contrasts *observing the law* over against twice concerning *justified by faith in Christ*.

The law can be viewed as serving a number of related purposes. First, it elucidates God's uncompromising standards. In particular, concerning our obligation to love God without reservation, and our neighbor as ourselves (cf. Matt. 22:37-40). Such as would require our diligent pursuit, often in the face of resilient obstacles.

Second, it reminds us of our failure in this regard. As succinctly expressed, "for all have sinned and fall short of the glory of God" (Rom. 3:23). As would sheep, who wander off.

Finally, it points us to God's resolution in Christ. "Where, then, is boasting?" Paul subsequently inquires. "On what principle? On that of observing the law? No, but on that of faith" (Rom. 3:27).

"You are all sons of God through faith in Christ Jesus," the apostle continues (3:26). They were also baptized into Christ—in keeping with what Oscar Brooks graphically describes as *the drama of decision*. In this regard, "Baptism is the concrete expression of a moral choice that has been made. It vividly portrays in time and space the inner decision made by the participant. John (and Jesus as well) has (have) carefully chosen a rite demanding participation."[2]

Paul next advances what might be considered a still more radical departure from conventional wisdom: "There is neither Jew nor Greek, slave nor free, male nor female, for you are all one in Christ Jesus" (3:28). This was obviously not meant to deny differences associated with ethnic origin, social status, or gender, but as applied to their unqualified acceptance within the household of faith.

In summary, the apostle declares: "For in Christ Jesus neither circumcision nor uncircumcision has any value" (5:6). In a manner of speaking, the playing field has been leveled for all concerned. As a result, it is not necessary for Gentile Christians to become Jewish proselytes in order to enjoy some special status.

Our attention now shifts to the Thessalonian epistles. Paul's ministry in Thessalonica had been productive, especially among the God-fearing Gentiles, before opposition forced him and Silas to move on. Now Timothy arrived with an essentially favorable progress report. There were exceptions, which the apostle sets out to address.

"For you, brothers, become imitators of God's churches in Judea, which are in Christ Jesus," Paul admonishes his readers (1 Thess. 2:14). Since they persevered in the face of persecution. In so doing, to enter into the sufferings of Christ, as an extension of his ministry.

Then, too, to experience Christ's consolation. In particular, to realize that they were not alone in their trial. Moreover, that God's grace is quite sufficient to endure any hardship—especially in the light of the Lord's promised return.

"Brothers," Paul fondly addresses them, "we do not want you to be ignorant about those who have fallen asleep, or to grieve like the rest of men, who have no hope"(1 Thess. 4:13). *Asleep* is an euphemistic way of referring to death.

The apostle shortly continues:

> For the Lord will come down from heaven, with a loud command, with the voice of the archangel and with the trumpet call of God, and the dead in Christ will rise first. After that, we who are still alive and are left will be caught up together with them in the clouds to meet the Lord in the air. And so we will be with the Lord forever.

Wherefore, comfort one anther with these words.

The Lord himself accents the continuity between Jesus' life and ministry and subsequent developments. *From heaven* alludes to the special place of God's abode and deliberation. It is here that Christ intercedes on behalf of those entrusting their ways to him. *The dead in Christ* are those who finish the course with resilient faith. These may expect to be forever with the Lord.

"Be joyful always," Paul admonishes them; "pray continually; give thanks in all circumstances, for this is God's will for you in Christ Jesus" (1 Thess. 5:16). "Some things vary in the Christian experience; they come and go. But some things have an 'always' attached to them. These verses almost certainly name three, for the explanatory clause at the end of these verses almost certainly refers to them all."[3]

Consequently, *be joyful always*—for this is God's will for you in Christ. Likewise, *pray continually*—for this too is God's will for you in Christ. Finally, *give thanks in all circumstances*—for this is no less God's will for you in Christ. At this propitious point, we take our leave of Paul's early correspondence.

Major Epistles

The apostle's major epistles include First and Second Corinthians, and Romans. Paul had spent an extensive period in the commercial center of Corinth. He now received a letter requiring a response. However, of seeming greater concern for him was troubling news from independent sources. Such as indicated that there was division and contention within the community.

"To the church of God in Corinth, to those sanctified in Jesus Christ and called to be holy," the apostle initiates his correspondence (1 Cor. 1:2).

> It might be assumed that a man who had such interest in justification would not have given much attention to sanctification, but Paul does not allow his exposition of justification to blind him to the need to reflect on man's quest for perfection. He did not see the doctrines as mutually exclusive, since one concerned man's relationship to God and the other the practical working out of what was already a *fait accompli* in Christ.[4]

As a result, one would readily gather that Paul assumed that those in Christ are works in progress.

"I always thank God for you because of his grace given you in Christ Jesus," the apostle subsequently confides (1:4). *Grace* implies unmerited favor. In what is perhaps the most cherished of hymns, John Newton exclaims:

> Amazing grace! How sweet the sound that saved a wretch like me!
> I once was lost, but now am found, was blind but now I see.
> Through many dangers, toils and snares I have already come;
> 'Tis grace that brought me safe thus far, and grace will lead me home.

"It is because of him (God) that you are in Christ Jesus," the apostle pointedly observes (1:30). It is not something one could have imagined, let alone deserve. Nevertheless, it is cause for rejoicing.

"Brothers, I could not address you as spiritual but as worldly," Paul later laments, "mere infants in Christ" (3:1). Such as might be expected of them when they were first converted, but not as mature believers. It would appear that the apostle thought that the Corinthians resembled rambunctious children, squabbling over inconsequential matters. In this condition, unable to help themselves, and ill-equipped to aid others.

"We are fools for Christ," Paul speaks on behalf of the apostles, "but you are so wise in Christ!" (4:10). *We are fools* in the sense of enduring ridicule, while endeavoring to disciple all peoples. Thus compounding their difficulties in furthering the gospel across cultural barriers.

You are so wise takes on a satirical mode, saying one thing to mean another. In that they attempt to reap where they have not sown. So also in that they court the acclaim of men, and thus have already received their reward (cf. Matt. 6:2).

"Even though you have ten thousand guardians in Christ," the apostle employs hyperbole, "you do not have many fathers, for in Christ Jesus I became your father through the gospel" (4:15). The analogy is apropos. Paul had sired them in the faith, while others might assist in the nurturing process or inhibit it.

In Christ or its equivalent is used three times in this brief passage. The repetition is by way of emphasis. In context, Paul earnestly reminds his readers that faith involves not simply belief but rigorous application. As popularly expressed, "One must not only talk the talk, but walk the walk."

"The grace of the Lord Jesus be with you," the apostle characteristically concludes. "My love to all of you in Christ Jesus. Amen" (16:23-24). *Grace* first since it is by this means that they embrace life in Christ. *Love* second in that it is necessary to sustain their calling. The two are coupled together as complementary in appropriating the Christian life.

Paul continues to monitor the situation at Corinth, resulting in additional correspondence. "But thanks be to God," he rejoices, "who always leads us in triumphant procession in Christ and through us spreads everywhere the fragrance of the knowledge of him" (2 Cor. 2:14).

What Paul has been saying up until this point in the letter could be taken as a rather depressing account of his ministry. He has spoken of affliction in Asia, criticism of his integrity, the pain experienced in Corinth because of the offender, and his inability to settle to missionary work in Troas. As if to balance this somewhat depressing account, Paul in these verses strikes a positive note, describing how God always and in every place enabled him to carry on an effective ministry despite the difficulties.[5]

In particular, he alludes to participating in a triumphant procession. Jesus Christ leads the procession, as the acclaimed victor over sin and death. Others follow, as tokens of his triumph. This, moreover, bringing to mind the sage saying, "All is well that ends well."

The apostle subsequently alludes to an occasion when Moses' face was veiled (cf. Exod. 34:33). "But their minds were made dull, for to this day the same veil remains when the old covenant is read," he comments. "It has not been removed, because only in Christ is it taken away" (3:14). He no doubt recalls his own experience in the synagogue, listening to the reading of Torah, but blinded by its glory. So the situation remained until in Christ the veil was removed.

"Therefore," seeing that Christ died for all, so that those who live should no longer live to themselves, "if anyone is in Christ, he is a new creation, the old has gone, the new has come!" (5:17). Since we touched on this text earlier, no elaboration would appear necessary.

"We have been speaking in the sight of God as those in Christ," Paul adamantly concludes, and everything we do, dear friends, is for your strengthening" (12:19). God is his witness.

As those in Christ, their concern must be to strengthen others in the faith. Instead of preying on their vulnerability, as was the custom of some. In this manner, helping them to achieve their full potential.

Paul had long hoped to visit the fellowship at Rome, but was hindered by some pressing matter or another (cf. Rom. 1:13). By way of reminder, it was said that all roads led to Rome. He continued to bear up the believers in prayer, in anticipation of soon visiting them. This would enable him to make a contribution to their individual and corporate life and ministry, in keeping with his apostolic calling and reflective of his missionary zeal.

Although all have fallen short of the glory of God, we may be "justified freely by his grace through the redemption in Christ" (3:24, free translation). The term *redemption* occurs only ten times in the New Testament: seven of these in the Pauline correspondence, twice in Hebrews (according to one tradition also authored by the apostle, and according to another *God only knows*—but then likely an associate of the apostle in his mission), and once by Luke.

The root meaning concerns the payment of a ransom. "For if, when we were God's enemies, we were reconciled to him through the death of his Son, how much more, having been reconciled, shall we be saved through his life!" (6:10). Having established the fact that we were enemies of Christ, Paul now are affirms that we are reconciled through his death as a ransom for sin.

"So also you count yourselves indeed dead to sin," he resolutely continues, "but living to God in Christ Jesus our Lord" (free translation). His exhortation is twofold: consider yourself *dead to sin*, so no longer under its control, and *living to God in Christ Jesus*. Consequently, do not pamper the former self with its degrading appetites, but nourish the new life with spiritual sustenance.

"For the wages of sin is death, but the gift of God is eternal life in Christ Jesus our Lord" (6:23).

> The contrast between sin and grace is now sharpened to a razor's edge.... The imagery of fruit is here abandoned for the military imagery of verse 13. Sin and God are depicted as warlords, the one paying the wages of death, the other offering release and freedom for life.[6]

"Therefore," given our deliverance from sin, "there is now no condemnation for those who are in Christ Jesus, because through Christ Jesus the law of the Spirit of life set me free from the law of sin and death" (8:1-2). For what the law was powerless to perform, those who live in accordance with the Spirit are freed from bondage.

The apostle speaks from experience. For what he would do, he found incapable of doing; and what he would not do, that he did (cf. 7:15). "Who will rescue me from this death?" he laments. "Thanks be to God—through Jesus Christ our Lord!" Through him and in him.

"Who shall separate us from the love of Christ?" Paul inquires further.

> Shall trouble or hardship or persecution or famine or nakedness or danger or sword?... No, in all these things we are more than conquerors through him who loved us. For I am convinced that neither death nor life, neither angels nor demons, neither the present nor the future, nor any powers, neither height nor depth, nor anything else in all creation, will be able to separate us from the love of God that is in Christ Jesus our Lord (8:35, 37-39).

"I speak the truth in Christ," the apostle subsequently asserts (9:1). As if he were on the witness stand. Then in all sincerity, without the slightest intention to deceive others or himself.

"Do not think of yourselves more highly than you ought, but rather think of yourself with sober judgment, in accordance with the measure of faith God has given you," he solemnly cautions. "Just as each of us has one body with many members, and these members do not all have the same function, so in Christ we who are many form one body" (12:3-5).

As for commentary, "Measurement by our own standards tends to result in a superiority complex, while measurement by the standards of others leads to an inferiority complex. Faith, on the other hand, always holds two things before the believers: we are sinners, but we are being redeemed by grace."[7]

Some serve in one way, and others in another. Both are necessary, and neither is to be depreciated. In whatever manner, God is to be glorified.

Paul singles out a number of individuals for personal greetings. For instance, "Greet Priscilla and Aquila, my fellow workers in Christ Jesus. They risked their lives for me. Not only I but all the churches of the Gentiles are grateful to them" (16:3). They were expelled from Rome, but had returned. Meanwhile, they endangered their lives on behalf of the community of faith.

The apostle would eventually reach Rome as a prisoner, having appealed his case to Caesar. He remained there for an extended period under what amounted to house arrest. It appears that he was subsequently released, only to be apprehended a second time and executed. If this reconstruction is accurate, his prison epistles appear to be written during his first imprisonment.

Prison Epistles

The prison epistles consist of Colossians, Ephesians, Philippians, and Philemon. No mention is made of Paul visiting Colossae, although there is speculation that he did so during his third missionary journey. Epaphras (cf. Col. 1:7) seems a likely candidate for having introduced the gospel in this setting. He later became a diligent co-worker with the apostle (cf. 4:13).

The occasion for Paul's epistle concerned a report from Epaphras that a false teaching was threatening the church.

> Basically, Paul is telling them that Christ has defeated the evil powers by his death on the cross (2:15). This means that the false teaching and enslaving regulations that come from human wisdom and from the ruling spirits of the universe (2:8) have no authority over the believers (2:10).[8]

"We always thank the Father of our Lord Jesus Christ, when we pray for you," the apostle appreciatively confides, "because we have heard of your faith in Christ Jesus and of the love you have for all the saints" (1:3-4). Such as was reported to him, as a means of encouragement and inciting prayer.

Faith and *love* are thus coupled together as a cherished legacy of being in Christ. *Faith* that what was preached to them was in fact true, and *love* as an evidence that God had begun a good work in them. Then, too, serving as tributaries to a *hope* "that is stored up for you in heaven." Bringing to mind his eloquent commentary, "And now these three remain: faith, hope and love. But the greatest of these is love" (1 Cor. 13:13).

"We proclaim him (Christ, the hope of glory)," the apostle continues, "admonishing and teaching everyone with all wisdom, so that we may present everyone perfect in Christ" (Col. 1:28). Note initially that the gospel is meant for all, and not some select few. Moreover, that it is for the purpose that they attain spiritual maturity. Otherwise expressed, that they conform to the perfect will of God in Christ.

"For though I am absent from you in body, I am present with you in spirit and delight to see how orderly you are and how firm your faith in Christ is" (2:5).

Although far removed, he enjoyed an intimate spiritual relationship. As evidenced by his rejoicing in the firmness of their faith.

Paul's letter to the Ephesians is thought to be a general encyclical, meant to expound on the cherished legacy of those who are in Christ. In this connection, to ground them in their newly acquired faith. The apostle sets forth his apostolic credentials at the outset (cf. Eph. 1:1), as if to formalize their relationship and anticipate his instruction.

They are a select community, determined by a common location. They are no less a segment of an universal fellowship, one that should present no barriers but only frontiers. As a result, that which would commend their faithfulness in Christ.

"Praise be to the God and Father of our Lord Jesus Christ," the apostle enthusiastically exclaims, "who has blessed us in the heavenly realms with every spiritual blessing in Christ" (1:3). "Spiritual blessings are to be distinguished, probably, from material blessings.... They include election to holiness, in statement as God's sons and daughters, redemption and forgiveness, the gift of the Spirit, and the hope of glory."[9]

"In him we were also chosen," Paul confidently continues,

> having been predestined according to the plan of him who works out everything in conformity with the purpose of his will, in order that we, who were the first to hope in Christ, might be for the praise of his glory. And you also were included in Christ when you heard the word of truth, the gospel of your salvation (1:11-13).

The first to hope in Christ may refer to Jewish believers. If so, *you also* would be the Gentile converts. In any case, all are on equal footing.

Where once we were subject to God's righteous wrath, now "because of his great love for us, God, who is rich in mercy, made us alive with Christ even when we were dead in transgressions—it is by grace you have been saved. And God raised us up with Christ and seated us with him in the heavenly realms in Christ Jesus" (2:4-6). As they were raised to newness of life, they were also to appropiate life in the Spirit.

This does not result from any merit on their part, but is solely by grace. Not grace set over against doing good, but grace resulting in doing good. Therefore,

> remember that formerly you who are Gentiles by birth ... (were) excluded from citizenship in Israel and foreigners to the covenants of the promise, without hope and without God in the world. But now in Christ Jesus you who once were far away have been brought near through the blood of Christ (2:11-13).

Cherish the new alternative, and make the most of it.

May God be justly honored for all that he has done. "Now to him who is able to do immeasurably more than all we ask or imagine, according to his power that is at work within us, to him be glory in the church and in Christ Jesus throughout all generations, for ever and ever! Amen" (3:20-21).

Be kind and compassionate to one another," the apostle admonishes, "forgiving each other, just as in Christ God forgave you" (4:22).

> Although there are few specific references to Paul's doctrine of forgiveness, the idea is basic to Paul's theology. Justification would be meaningless if the justified man had no assurance that his sins were forgiven. Similarly, reconciliation with God would be equally unintelligible if the burden of guilt were not removed.[10]

Forgiveness is contingent on repentance. A turning away from sin, and turning toward the Almighty. From beginning to end, it is a process negotiated in Christ. Paul does not mean to leave the issue in doubt.

"If then any comfort in Christ, if any consolation of love, if any fellowship of spirit, if any compassion and pity," the apostle admonishes the Philippians, "fulfill my joy, that you be like-minded, having the same love, being one in spirit and purpose" (Phil. 2:1-2, free translation). He thus appeals on the basis of the comfort they have experienced in Christ.

He also pleads for unanimity, so that his joy might be made complete. This does not preclude differences of opinion, but submits them to a common purpose. So that they might seek to glorify God in all that is said and done.

"What is more," Paul shortly continues,

> I consider everything a loss compared to the surpassing greatness of knowing Christ Jesus my Lord, for whose sake I have lost all things. I consider them rubbish, that I may gain Christ and be found in him, not having a righteousness of my own that comes form the law, but that which is through faith in Christ—the righteousness that comes from God and is by faith (3:7-9).

"The knowledge of God was of paramount value in the eyes of the great prophets of Israel; for Paul the knowledge of God was supremely mediated through Christ, and in being so mediated it was immensely enriched."[11]

"Not that I have already obtained all this," the apostle confesses,

> or have already been made perfect, but I press on to take hold of that for which Christ Jesus took hold of me. . . . But one thing I do: Forgetting what is behind and straining toward what is ahead, I press on toward the goal to win the prize for which God has called me heavenward in Christ Jesus (3:12-14).

With singular devotion, he presses on in Christ.

"And my God will meet all your needs according to his glorious riches in Christ Jesus," Paul enthusiastically concludes. "Greet all the saints in Christ Jesus" (4:19, 21). In a magnanimous fashion, in keeping with a generous spirit.

The apostle also writes a letter to Philemon concerning a runaway slave named *Onesimus*. He urges he be accepted back, not as a slave but a beloved brother in the Lord. "Therefore (given the good report he has heard of Philemon), although in Christ I could be bold and order you to do what you ought to do, yet I appeal to you on the basis of love" (v. 8).

The best way to approximate what this verse means is to see it in the context of the letter as teaching these truths: All Christians share a common faith; faith should be an active faith because it promotes an understanding of the blessings believers have received, the response of faith is for Christ, that is, for his glory.[12]

Since *all Christians share a common faith*, they are bonded together and obligated for one another.

In addition, *faith should be active*. Not in a legalistic fashion, as if to render service for service, but in terms of a generous lifestyle. In this manner, each attempt to excel in a common cause.

This is not for the purpose of promoting self, but so that Christ might be glorified. In that persons will recognize that they are his disciples, bent on serving his purposes, and activated by his spirit.

"Epaphras, my fellow prisoner in Christ Jesus, sends you greetings," the apostle adds (1:23). While a seemingly casual reference, it epitomizes the centrality of being in Christ from Paul's perspective. As such, that which invests life with meaning, and solicits a believing response.

Pastoral Epistles

The pastoral epistles embrace First and Second Timothy and Titus.

While the title is not technically quite correct in that the Epistles do not deal with pastoral duties in the sense of the care of souls, yet is popularly appropriate as denoting the essentially practical nature of the subject matter as distinguished from the other Epistles attributed to Paul.[13]

Timothy was a younger associate of Paul. The apostle describes him as "my true son in the faith" (1 Tim. 1:2). In popular idiom, "One that does his papa proud." In his role as mentor, Paul admonishes him: "Don't let anyone look down on you because you are young, but set an example for the believers in speech, in life, in love, in faith and in purity" (1 Tim. 4:12).

Titus is also actively engaged with Paul and Timothy in the ministry. In similar fashion, he is described as "my true son" (Titus 1:4). The duties assigned to him seem to be of more general nature. As an example, "Remind the people to be subject to rulers and authorities, to be obedient, to be ready to do whatever is good, to slander no one, to be peaceable and considerate, and to show true humility toward all men" (3:3).

"The grace of our Lord was poured out on me abundantly," the apostle enthuses, "along with the faith and love that are in Christ Jesus" (1 Tim. 1:14). He appears to be caught up in the wonder of it all. His cup overflows. What he has experienced for himself, he would commend to others.

Faith and *love* parallel *goodness* and *love* (alternatively translated *mercy*) in the Psalter (cf. 23:6). In the former instance, they resemble two guard dogs who keep the flock from going astray, and protect them from assault. Consequently, "Those who have served well gain an excellent standing and great assurance in their faith in Christ Jesus" (3:13).

An excellent understanding likely refers to their reputation in the community. In this regard, "A good name is more desirable than great riches; to be esteemed is better than silver or gold" (Prov. 22:1). Conversely, they are not to covet the acclaim of men, but the approval of God.

"Paul, an apostle of Christ Jesus by the will of God," the apostle prefaces his second epistle to Timothy, "according to the promise of the life that is in Christ Jesus" (1:1). He thus affirms his apostolic office; hence, the authoritative character of his message. This, in turn, solicits their faithful compliance.

According to the promise of life clarifies the purpose for which his apostolic office was designed. He thereby implies that the quality of life improves immeasurably for those in Christ. Since they are the recipients of God's lavish blessing, and the benefits of life together.

"What you have heard from me," the apostle continues, "keep as the pattern of sound teaching, with faith and love in Christ Jesus" (1:13). He characteristically sets *sound teaching* over against *false teachers*. *Faith* and *love* again appear in context of being in Christ, by way of emphasis and assurance. Throughout life and so as to guide the believer into a safe harbor.

"You, then, my son, be strong in the grace that is in Christ Jesus. And the things you have heard me say in the presence of many witnesses entrust to reliable men who will also be qualified to teach others" (2:1). *Grace* is employed in an instrumental sense, bringing to mind Paul's confident assertion: "I can do all things through him who gives me strength" (Phil. 4:13).

He, moreover, admonishes him to *be strong*. Consequently, to appropriate that which God has provided. Then to pass on the cherished legacy from one generation to the next.

"Therefore (since God's word remains unfettered) I endure everything for the sake of the elect, that they too may obtain the salvation that is in Christ Jesus, with eternal glory" (2:10). It goes without saying that *everything* allows for no exceptions.

So that they might experience deliverance in Christ. Deliverance from the powers and principalities of this world, and deliverance from the insatiable lusts of the flesh as well. Conversely, free to embrace God and others. Consequently, to live above reproach.

This is associated with *eternal glory*, such as will be revealed with Jesus' triumphant return. So that they live toward the future, having already received an earnest of things to come. Thus undaunted by obstacles and opposition.

"In fact," the apostle concludes, "everyone who wants to live a godly life in Christ Jesus will be persecuted" (3:12). As a natural consequence, not meant to apply equally to all situations (cf. 1 Peter 4:12-13). Nor should it necessarily be assumed as a mark of spirituality.

We have thus seen that the expression *in Christ* embodies rich and varied nuances. It is sometimes employed in the context of personal devotion; in other instances, regarding life together; on still other occasions, in anticipation of the future. Whether explicit or implicit, it is never far from Paul's reflection.

It, moreover, is used to encourage believers in the face of relentless opposition and merciless persecution. Then as a means of consolation at the loss of a loved one. In subtle ways, such as a simple greeting. All things considered, as a constant point of reference in the midst of changing circumstances.

Thus concludes our first exploration into an entreating topic. Not only has it made a vital contribution in itself, but paves the way for the discussion to follow.

JESUS OF HISTORY

If the much heralded quest for the Jesus of history has taught us anything, it should be that the Christ of faith is meaningless when taken out of context. Therefore, it is proper that we sketch the life and ministry of Jesus as relevant for the topic at hand. I will do so briefly, so not to unnecessarily labor the point.

What seems conspicuously down-played in the expansive literature is the critical importance of Luke's account, which is deserving of the designation *the original quest*.[1] Having taken study groups to Israel on various occasions, and lived there for four years, I am amazed at how readily one can reconstruct the events from his narrative. This, in turn, recalls his revealing prologue:

> Many have undertaken to draw up an account of the things that have been fulfilled among us, just as they were handed down to us by those who from the first were eyewitness and servants of the word. Therefore, since I myself have carefully investigated everything from the beginning, it seemed good also to me to write an orderly account for you, most excellent Theophilus, so that you may know the certainty of the things you have been taught (1:1-4).

He apparently makes reference to oral tradition, to which he has given careful attention. This resulted in an orderly account, one that with little exception follows a chronological order. *Theophilus* could be a recent convert, and/or patron, or simply a personification of one that loves God.

Not to be overlooked, Luke constitutes the first of a two-volume work: concerning the life and ministry of Jesus, and the acts of the apostles. These serve to explain how a seemingly inconsequential Jewish sect became a faith with cosmopolitan appeal in an exceedingly brief period of time. So it is that we turn to Luke as our guide.

The Early Years

God sent his angel Gabriel to a virgin pledged to be married, who was named *Mary*.

You will be with child and give birth to a son, and you are to give him the name Jesus. He will be great and will be called the Son of the Most High. The Lord God will give him the throne of his father David, and he will reign over the house of Jacob forever; his kingdom will never end (1:31-33).

Now a decree went out that a census should be taken throughout the entire Roman Empire. So Joseph went up from Nazareth to Bethlehem, since he belonged to the line of David. Mary, who was expecting, accompanied him. While there, Mary gave birth to a son, who she wrapped in cloths and placed him in a manger—since there was no room for them in the inn.

There were shepherds living out in the fields nearby, keeping watch over their flocks at night. An angel of the Lord appeared to them, the glory of the Lord shone around them, and they were terrified. "Do not be afraid," the angel assured them. "I bring you good news of great joy that will be for all people. Today in the town of David a Savior has been born to you; he is Christ the Lord" (2:10-11).

Suddenly a great company of the heavenly host appeared with the angel, praising God and saying: "Glory to God in the highest, and on earth peace to men on whom his favor rests." When the angels took their leave, the shepherds hurried off to see the child. After that, they returned to their duties, glorifying and praising God.

Luke next notes two ritual ceremonies, one concerning the presentation of the child and the other regarding the purification of its mother (cf. 2:21-22). As for the former, "The first offspring of every womb among the Israelites belongs to me, whether man or animal" (Exod. 13:2). Such could be redeemed from service by a nominal fee.

As for the latter,

> The Levitical law provided that after the birth of a son a woman would be unclean for seven days and that for a further thirty-three days she should keep away from all holy things (cf. Lev. 12:1-5) Then she should offer a lamb and a dove or pigeon. If she was too poor for a lamb a second dove or pigeon sufficed instead.[2]

Since Joseph and Mary presented the lesser of the sacrifices, we can assume that they were of modest means.

Simeon was a righteous and devout person living in Jerusalem. It had been revealed to him that he would not die before he had see *the Lord's Christ*. Taking the child in his arms, he praised God saying: "Sovereign Lord, as you have promised, you now dismiss your servant in peace. For my eyes have seen your salvation, which you have prepared in the sight of all people, a light for revelation to the Gentiles, and for glory to your people Israel."

There was also a prophetess named *Anna*. She worshiped in the temple night and day. Coming upon them, she gave thanks to God and spoke concerning the child *to all who were looking forward to the redemption of Jerusalem*.

When Joseph and Mary had fulfilled their religious obligations, they returned to Nazareth. There Jesus *grew and became strong, was filled with wisdom*, and *the grace of God was upon him.* That is to say, he matured in every way, as one would hope for a child of the covenant.

When Jesus was twelve years of age, the family again went up to Jerusalem—to observe the Passover. When it came time for them to return, they supposed that Jesus was with relatives or friends. After a day's travel, they went looking for him, but he was nowhere to be found. They then retraced their steps to Jerusalem, and after three days found him in the temple courts. He was sitting among the rabbis, listening to them and asking questions. People were amazed by his insight.

"Son, why have you treated us like this?" Mary inquired of him. "Your father and I have been anxiously searching for you" (2:48).

"Why were you searching for me?" he replied. "Didn't you know I had to be in my Father's house?" These are the first words of Jesus recorded by Luke, as if to lay the course he would take in life.

Once again, they returned to Nazareth—where Jesus was subject to his parents. Luke perhaps mentions this in order not to give the wrong impression from the preceding interchange. The portrait we get is that of a precocious and devout lad. One who honors his parents, and faithfully assumed his responsibilities. Quite unlike later fanciful accounts, such as that of Jesus coming to the assistance of Joseph—who had cut two boards of differing lengths. "Put the two boards down and line them up at one end," Jesus was reported to have said. Whereupon, he grasped the shorter board, and stretched it until the two were the same length.[3]

His Public Ministry

John the Baptist inaugurated his public ministry prior to that of Jesus. He went into the region around the Jordan, preaching a baptism of repentance for the forgiveness of sins. People wondered if he were the Messiah, but he insisted that it was his role to prepare the way.

Jesus came along with others to be baptized. Then, as he was praying, heaven opened and the Holy Spirit descended on him in the likeness of a dove. So also a voice came from heaven: "You are my Son, whom I love; with you I am well pleased" (3:22).

"Jesus, full of the Holy Spirit, returned from the Jordan and was led by the Spirit in the desert (wilderness), where he was tempted by the devil" (4:1). "If you are the son of God," the devil impugned, "tell this stone to become bread."

"It is written," Jesus replied: "'Man does not live on bread alone'" (cf. Deut. 8:3). The temptation continued, with similar results. Then the devil took leave of him, until some more convenient time. Jesus had withstood the efforts to divert him from his appointed task.

He then returned to Galilee *in the power of the Spirit*, and news concerning him spread throughout the countryside. He taught in the synagogues, where he was well received. Initially, nothing is said of his performing miracles.

He made his way to Nazareth, and went to the synagogue—as was his custom. He stood to read, and the Isaiah scroll was handed to him. Unrolling it, he found the place where it was written: "The Spirit of the Lord is on me, because he has anointed me to reach good news to the poor. He has sent me to proclaim freedom for the prisoners and recovery of sight for the blind, to release the oppressed, to proclaim the year of the Lord's favor" (4:18-19: cf. Isa. 61:1-2). He stopped pointedly short of the reference to "the day of the vengeance of our God."

This constituted Jubilee imagery applied to the Messianic Age. *Jubilee* was a time for emancipation and restoration, meant to be observed every fiftieth year. It recognized God's sovereignty; and, as its corollary, the sharing of his benevolence. As an example, debts were forgiven and land taken in payment returned to its original owner.

After reading from the scroll, Jesus sat down in preparation for teaching. The eyes of everyone were riveted on him. He began by say, "Today this scripture is fulfilled in your hearing."

The people were incensed at his subsequent criticism of their intransigence, and rushed him to the top of a hill—with the intent to cast him down. However, he walked through their midst, and went his way. Luke provides no details. If it was a miracle, it was decidedly not the kind they would have preferred.

Jesus then went down to Capernaum, and on the Sabbath began to teach the people. "They were amazed with his teaching, because his message had authority" (4:32). Unlike that of the rabbis, who relied heavily on precedent.

There was in the synagogue a man possessed by a demon. Jesus ordered it to come out of him. When the demon complied, the people were duly impressed. "What is this teaching?" they inquired. "With authority and power he gives orders to evil spirits and they come out!" (4:36). After that, Jesus healed many others.

One day as he was standing by the Sea of Galilee, teaching the people crowded around him, he saw two boats left by the fishermen who were washing their nets. He got into the one owned by Simon Peter, and asked him to put out a little from the shore—making it easier for him to be heard.

When he had finished, he urged Peter to put out into the deep water—in anticipation of a good catch. Peter protested, seeing they had labored all night without success. When he did as Jesus bid him, the nets held so many fish that they signaled their partners to assist them. Whereupon, both boats threatened to sink.

"Don't be afraid," Jesus encouraged Peter; "from now on you will catch men" (5:19). So they pulled their boats up on shore, left everything, and followed him.

Two additional healing episodes follow, one concerning a man suffering from leprosy and the other a paralytic. The former illustrates Jesus' willingness to approach outcasts, while being sensitive to the need to be accepted back into society.

After this, Jesus saw a tax collector named *Levi* at his tax booth. "Follow me," Jesus enjoined him, and he got to his feet, left everything and followed Jesus (5:27). Now Levi prepared a banquet for Jesus and many tax collectors and others were eating with them. However, certain Pharisees complained to his disciples, "Why do you eat and drink with collectors and 'sinners' (non-observant Jews)?" As for commentary,

With their strict rules of ceremonial purity it was unthinkable that they would have eaten with people such as Levi and his associates. Some members of such a company were bound to be ceremonially unclean and there was no surer way of contracting defilement than by associating with *sinners*. Moreover to eat with a man meant friendship, full acceptance.[4]

Jesus answered them, "It is not the healthy who need a doctor, but the sick. I have not come to call the righteous, but sinners to repentance."

On another occasion, Jesus went out on a mountainside and spent the entire night in prayer. When morning came, he called his disciples to him and chose twelve of them—whom he designated as *apostles*. Likely meant to recall the twelve tribes of Israel, they were singled out to carry on Jesus' ministry as his bequest and via his enablement.

After that, he made his way down to a level place and declared:

Blessed are you who are poor, for yours is the kingdom of God. Blessed are you who hunger now, for you will be satisfied. Blessed are you who weep now, for you will laugh. Blessed are you when men hate you, when they exclude you and insult you and reject your name as evil, because of the Son of Man (6:20-22).

"Love your enemies," Jesus enjoined them, "do good to those who hate you, bless those who curse you, pray for those who mistreat you" (6:27-28). If someone strikes you on one check (likely with the back of the hand, as an insult), turn the other to him also. "Do to others as you would have them do to you."

He traveled from one village to another, "proclaiming the good news of the kingdom of God" (8:1).

Although Judaism expected an eschatological kingdom there was no conception that this kingdom would break into the present except to bring the present to an end. The fact that Jesus taught men to expect a kingdom in the present while the existing situation continued produced a new element into current expectations.[5]

"Who do the crowds say I am?" Jesus inquired of his disciples (9:18).

They replied, "Some say John the Baptist, others say Elijah, and still others, that one of the prophets of long ago has come back to life." This would imply that they thought him associated with the prophetic tradition, but had difficulty sorting out the relationship.

"What about you?" Jesus asked them. "Who do you say I am?"

Peter adamantly answered, "The Christ (Anointed) of God." He perhaps meant to speak on behalf of the other apostles.

Jesus then cautions them not to prematurely divulge this to the populace. In this regard, "The Son of Man must suffer many things and be rejected by the elders, chief priests and teachers of the law, and he must be killed and on the third day be raised to life." Whereupon, they would be witnesses to these events.

About eight days later, Jesus took Peter, John, and James with him up a mountain to pray. As he was praying, his countenance became radiant. Moses and Elijah, representing the law and prophets, appeared in glorious splendor with him. They conversed regarding his coming demise.

As the visitors were about to take their leave, Peter suggested constructing booths for Jesus and the others. He was perhaps thinking in terms of the Feast of Tabernacles. By way of elaboration,

> On Sukkoth we give thanks for our redemption from Egypt and for God's providence during the many years of wandering through the desert. By dwelling in an exposed, insecure hut, we are reminded that true security comes from being sheltered under God's protective wings.[6]

After that, a voice from heaven declared: "This is my Son, whom I have chosen; listen to him." When the voice had spoken, Jesus stood alone—as if to assume center stage.

Jerusalem Bound

"As the time approached for him to be taken up, Jesus resolutely set out for Jerusalem" (9:51, free translation). He sent messengers on ahead, into a Samaritan village to prepare for his arrival. Its inhabitants did not welcome him, because he was on his way to worship in Jerusalem—a practice which they emphatically disapproved.

"Lord," James and John inquired, "do you want us to call fire down from heaven to destroy them?" They perhaps had in mind the occasion when Elijah called down fire from heaven on the soldiers of Ahaziah (cf. 2 Kings 1:9-16). Jesus rebuked them, and they went on to another village.

As they were walking along the road, a certain man confided in Jesus: "I will follow you wherever you go" (9:57).

Jesus replied, "Foxes have holes and birds of the air have nests, but the Son of Man has no place to lay his head." This he said by way of emphasizing the cost of discipleship. He then exhorted another, "Follow me."

"Lord," the man responded, "first let me go and bury my father." In other words, initially fulfill his family obligations.

"Let the dead bury their own dead," Jesus countered, "but you go and proclaim the kingdom of God. "Let those without spiritual insight perform the duties they can do so well; burial is very much in keeping for the spiritually dead. But the man who has seen the vision must not deny or delay his heavenly calling."[7]

Still another said, "I will follow you, Lord; but first let me go back and say good-by to my family." This appears to imply some equivocation on his part.

Jesus replied, "No one who puts his hand to the plow and looks back is fit for service in the kingdom of God." If one is to plow a straight furrow, he must keep his eyes fixed ahead.

"Teacher," *an expert in the law* inquired of Jesus, "what must I do to inherit eternal life?" (10:25).

"What is written in the Law?" he responded. "How do you read (interpret) it?"

He answered, "'Love the Lord your God with all your heart and with all your soul and with all your strength and with all your mind'; and, 'Love your neighbor as yourself'" (cf. Deut. 6:5; Lev. 19:18).

"You have answered correctly," Jesus commended him. "Do this and you will live."

He, wanting to justify himself, inquired: "And who is my neighbor?"

In response, Jesus told a story concerning a man accosted by thieves, who beat and left him in critical condition. A priest came along, but upon seeing the stricken person, passed by on the other side of the road. After that, a Levite came along, but also ignored plight of the victim. Then, finally, a Samaritan came along, ministered to the man, and took him to an inn where he could recover. "Which of these three do you think was a neighbor to the man who fell into the hands of robbers?" Jesus pointedly asked.

"The one who had mercy on him," the inquirer responded.

Jesus exhorted him, "Go and do likewise."

Tax collectors and *sinners* where gathering around to hear his teaching. This solicited a complaint from certain of the Pharisees, "This man welcomes sinners and eats with them" (15:2). Jesus responded with three parables: concerning a lost sheep, coin, and son. For instance, "Suppose one of you has a hundred sheep and loses one of them. Does he not leave the ninety-nine in the open country and go after the lost sheep until he finds it?" Then he rejoices with his neighbors. "I tell you that in the same way there will be more rejoicing in heaven over one sinner who repents than over ninety-nine righteous persons who do not need to repent."

Continuing on his way to Jerusalem, Jesus entered into a certain village (cf. 17:11). There he encountered ten lepers, who stood at a distance and cried out: "Jesus, Master, have pity on us!"

"Go," he responded, "show yourselves to the priests." This would confirm their cleansing, and allow them to be accepted back into society. One of them turned back, prostrated himself at Jesus' feet and thanked him, and he was a Samaritan.

"Were not all ten cleansed?" Jesus inquired. "Where are the other nine? Was no one found to return and give praise to God except this foreigner?"

Jesus subsequently told a parable by way of admonishing "some who were confident of their own righteousness and looked down on everybody else" (18:9). It seems that two men went to the temple to pray, one a Pharisee and the other a tax collector. The Pharisee stood boldly to his feet, and prayed concerning himself: "God, I thank you that I am not like other men—robbers, evildoers, adulterers—or even like this tax collector. I fast twice a week and give a tenth of all I get."

In contrast, the tax collector stood at a respectful distance, would not even look up to heaven, but beat his breast. "God," he pled, "have mercy on me, a 'sinner'."

"I tell you," Jesus solemnly declared, "This man, rather than the other, went home justified before God. For everyone who exalts himself will be humbled, and he who humbles himself will be exalted."

Jesus had crossed back over the Jordan River, and was passing through Jericho. There was a man there named *Zacchaeus*, a chief tax collector and wealthy. Since he was small of stature, he had difficulty seeing over the people who lined the way. So he ran ahead, and limbed up into a sycamore-fig tree in order to view the procession. "Zacchaeus," Jesus addressed him, "come down immediately. I must stay at your house today" (19:5). Whereupon, the chief tax collector provided hospitality.

"Look, Lord!" he subsequently exclaimed. "Here and now I give half of my possessions to the poor, and if I have cheated anybody out of anything, I will pay back for times the amount."

"Today," Jesus said in response, "salvation has come to this house because this man, too, is a son of Abraham. For the Son of Man is come to seek and to save what was lost." This instance provides a fitting transition into the passion account.

Passion Narrative

Luke breezes through Jesus' early years, takes a more deliberate approach to his public ministry, and dwells at length on his passion. When the entourage came near the place where the road dips down the Mount of Olives into the Kidron Valley, Jesus' disciples began to joyfully praise God in loud voices for all the miracles they had witnessed. "Blessed is the king who comes in the name of the Lord!" they cried out. "Peace in heaven and glory in the highest!"

"Teacher," some of the Pharisees enjoined Jesus, "rebuke your disciples!"

"I tell you," he replied, "if they keep quiet, the stones will cry out." It was likely a proverbial saying, perhaps derived from the idea of a pile of stones bearing witness (cf. Gen. 31:48).

He subsequently entered the temple precinct, and began driving out those using it for commercial purposes (cf. 19:45). "My house will be a house of prayer," he reminded them. "But you have made it a den of robbers" (cf. Isa. 56:7; Jer. 7:11). It was a largely symbolic act, calculated to invite the rage of the religious establishment.

Jesus continued to teach in the temple precincts, while the authorities sought an occasion to bring charges against him. As Jesus looked up, he saw the rich putting their ample gifts into the temple treasure. He also saw a poor widow cast in two small copper coins. "I tell you the truth," he solemnly affirmed, "this poor widow has put in more than all the others. All these people gave their gifts out of their wealth; but she out of her poverty put in all she had to live on" (21:3-4). Thus we would gather that generosity is not measured by what one gives, but by how much is left.

Some of Jesus' disciples were remarking about the beauty of the temple. "As for what you see here," he observed, "the time will come when not one stone will be left on another; every one of them will be thrown down" (21:6).

"Teacher," they inquired, "when will these things happen? And what will be the sign that they are about to take place?" They apparently associated this with the consummation of the age.

Jesus seized on this opportunity to distinguish between the two. As for the former, "When you see Jerusalem being surrounded by armies, you will know that its desolation is near. Then let those who are in Judea flee to the mountains, let those in the city get out, and let those in the country not enter into the city" (21:20-21). As for the latter, Jesus depicts a time of cosmic upheaval.

"Go and make preparations for us to eat the Passover," Jesus instructed Peter and John (22:8). When they had inclined at the table, he took bread, giving thanks and saying: "This is my body given for you; do this in remembrance of me." In the same way, he took the cup, adding: "This cup is the new covenant in my blood, which is poured out for you."

As for commentary,

> it seems clear that Jesus instituted the Lord's Supper by associating it with the third cup of wine, which came after the Passover meal was eaten. It was known as the "cup of redemption." ... He refused, however, to drink the fourth cup, referred to as the "cup of consummation." The unfinished meal of Jesus was a pledge that redemption would be consummated at (a) future messianic banquet.[8]

After the meal, Jesus *went out as usual* to the Mount of Olives. Matthew and Mark identify this as *Gethsemane*, indicative of an olive press. "Pray that you will not enter into temptation," Jesus urged his disciples (22:40).

He withdrew about a stone's throw, knelt down, and fervently prayed: "Father, if you are willing, take this cup from me; yet not my will, but yours be done." Being in anguish, he prayed more intently, and his perspiration resembled drops of blood falling to the ground.

When Jesus returned to his disciples, he found them asleep—*exhausted from sorrow*. "Why are you sleeping" he asked them. "Get up and pray so that you will not fall into temptation."

While he was still speaking, Judas arrived with those instructed to apprehend him. Peter offered resistance, but Jesus rebuked him. "Am I leading a rebellion, that you come with swords and clubs?" he protested. "Every day I was with you in the temple court, and you did not lay a hand on me. But this is your hour—when darkness reigns." They led him away to the residence of the high priest.

Peter followed at a distance. Then, when challenged, he denied Christ. He wept bitterly. Moreover, they were tears of repentance.

The soldiers mocked and abused Jesus. At daybreak he was taken before the Sanhedrin. He was asked whether he was in fact the Christ. "If I tell you, you will not believe me," Jesus replied, "and if I asked you, you would not answer. But from now on, the Son of Man will be seated at the right hand of the mighty God" (22:67-69). They concluded that he had incriminated himself.

They led him away to stand before the Roman magistrate Pilate. "We have found this man subverting the nation," they accused him (23:2). Conversely, Pilate found no basis for the charge against him.

They insisted, "He stirs up the people all over Judea by his teaching. He started in Galilee and has come all the way here."

When Pilate learned he was from Galilee, he sent him off to Herod—who was in Jerusalem at the time. Herod was pleased to see Jesus, since he had heard many things concerning him, and hoped he might perform some miracle. He plied him with many questions, which Jesus chose not to answer. Then they mocked Jesus, dressed him in an elegant robe in derision, and sent him back to Pilate.

Pilate then offered to have Jesus punished, and release him. "But with loud shouts they insistently demanded that he be crucified, and their shouts prevailed." Pilate no doubt concluded that keeping the peace and consolidating his position was of more consequence than serving justice.

They led Jesus away to be crucified. A large number of people followed him, including women who mourned and wailed for him. "Daughters of Jerusalem," Jesus addressed them, "do not weep for me; weep for yourselves and for your children. . . . For if men do these things when the tree is green, what will happen when it is dry?" (23:28, 31). Thus he affirmed his own innocense.

Two other men, both criminals, were also led out with him to be executed. When they came to a place called the Skull, they crucified them. "Father," Jesus petitioned, "forgive them, for they do not know what they are doing."

The people stood watching. "He saved others," the religious authorities ridiculed him; "let him save himself if he is the Christ of God, the Chosen One."

The soldiers perfunctorily offered Jesus a mixture of wine and vinegar to ease his suffering. "If you are the king of the Jews," they reasoned, "save yourself." This was in reference to the notice affixed above Jesus' head, which read *The King of the Jews*. It appears as his only crime.

"Aren't you the Christ?" one of the criminals protested. "Save yourself and save us!"

"Don't you fear God," the other responded, "since we are under the same sentence? We are punished justly, for we are getting what our deeds deserve. But this man has done nothing wrong." Turning to Jesus, he pled "remember me when you come into your kingdom."

"I tell you the truth," Jesus confidently replied, "today you will be with me in paradise."

Luke's account of Jesus' demise contains "three elements: the exceptional signs that preceded it, the death itself, and the responses of those witnessing it. Darkness shrouded the earth from noon to three in the afternoon. It was as if primal chaos had returned."[9] In a figurative sense, it had.

The curtain of the temple was also rent in two. This would signify that access to God was made available. God, it would seem, is disposed to employ object lessons to convey spiritual truths.

Jesus cried out with a loud voice: "Father, into your hands I commit my spirit." With this, he breathed his last. He had completed the task assigned to him. His suffering was over. He rested confident of the future.

The centurion, having witnessed all that had transpired, praised God and concluded: "Surely this was a righteous man." The people beat their breasts, as a sign of remorse, and went their way. Joseph, a member of the Sanhedrin, requested the body of Jesus to give it a proper burial. His body was wrapped and laid in a tomb. Women went to prepare spices and perfumes to anoint the corpse once the Sabbath was over.

On the first day of the week, very early in the morning, the women took the spices they had prepared, and went to the tomb. They found the stone rolled away, and the body was nowhere to be found. As they were pondering what might have happened, two radiant figures stood beside them. "Why do look for the living among they dead?" they inquired. "He is not here; he has risen!" (24:5).

Now the same day two of the disciples were making their way to a village called *Emmaus*, about seven miles from Jerusalem. As they were walking along, Jesus joined them, but they were kept from recognizing him. It was only later, with the breaking of bread, that they realized who he was.

Still later, Jesus appeared to the Eleven. "Peace be with you," Jesus declared (24:36). They were frightened, and supposed they saw a ghost. Conversely, Jesus assured them: "This is what I told you while I was still with you. Everything must be fulfilled that is written about me in the Law of Moses, the Prophets and the Psalms (the threefold division of the Hebrew canon)."

He subsequently urged them to remain in Jerusalem until the outpouring of the Holy Spirit. When he had led them out to the vicinity of Bethany, he lifted up his hands and blessed them. As he was doing so, he ascended into heaven. They joyfully returned to Jerusalem, and stayed continually in the Temple—praising God.

CHRIST OF FAITH

Sandwiched between the old (first) and new (second) quest for the historical Jesus was an era alternatively described as the *no biography* or *Christ of faith* era. The old quest had floundered, since the reconstructions differed in so marked fashion from one another, and sometimes even within themselves.

It remained to shift the emphasis from the Jesus of history to the Christ of faith. Rudolph Bultmann emerged as the leading proponent of this approach. He held

> that Jesus' teaching did not center around such ideas as the infinite worth of personality, the cultivation of the inner life, the development of man toward an ideal; that Jesus spoke rather of the coming Kingdom of God, which was to be God's gift, not man's achievement, of man's decision for or against the Kingdom, and of the divine demand for obedience.[1]

In other words, he opted for an existential interpretation of the text. One whose concern was not with a detailed account of Jesus' life or his moral teaching, but a faith encounter with the exigencies of life.

In doing so, he supposed that we can dispose of the archaic mentality thought no longer acceptable to modern man. This was identified as *demythologizing*. It, in turn, created a related problem. As expressed by one of Bultmann's students, "Now that we have demythologized the Bible, who is going to demythologize the professor?"

What then? The pendulum would swing back in the other direction—toward the Jesus of history. Not all the way, to be sure; but enough to realize that what we can know about the life and teachings of Jesus is of critical importance to negotiating the Christ of faith.

Apart from Paul, the other apostles had been with Jesus from *the beginning*: associated with the ministry of John and eventuating with that of Jesus. They were for the most part Galileans. They could recall walking with Jesus through the fields adorned with spring flowers, and birds flying overhead. These were pleasant times!

They could also remember making their way through the Arbel Pass, with its imposing cliffs looking down on them. Perhaps they recalled how military forces had come that way in times past. They were bent on a greater mission. These were challenging times!

Jesus' passion would assuredly be riveted in their memories. The darkness that seemed to engulf them on that occasion, along with Jesus' resolute determination. Death was swallowed up in victory. It was redemptive time!

As a result, they must have had relatively little difficulty making the connection between the Jesus of history and Christ of faith. The past was still very much with them, even though they had to negotiate changing circumstances. Not so with the apostle Paul. What he knew of Jesus, he learned from others. Furthermore, this was distorted by the antagonism of his associates.

According to his own testimony,

> he associated himself with Stephen's accusers, guarding the outer garments of his witnesses as, in conformity with the ancient law, they threw the first stones at his execution. Then he took part enthusiastically in the campaign of repression against the church of Jerusalem, . . . arresting and imprisoning men and women, endeavoring to make them renounce their faith when they were brought before synagogue courts, and pursuing refugees beyond the frontiers of Judea in an attempt to bring them back to face trial and punishment.[2]

Saul, "still breathing out murderous threats against the Lord's disciples," secured authorization from the high priest to apprehend any of Jesus' followers in Damascus, and bring them back as prisoners to Jerusalem (Acts 9:1-2). As he neared his destination, suddenly a bright light flashed around him. He fell to the ground, and heard a voice from heaven address him: "Saul, Saul, why do you persecute me?"

"Who are you Lord?" he inquired.

"I am Jesus, whom you are persecuting," the voice continued. "Now get up and go into the city, and you will be told what you must do."

He made two related discoveries.

> First, the Christians had been right in proclaiming the resurrection of Jesus. The use of his name here expresses Paul's realization that the Jesus of history was the Christ of this appearance. Second, Gamaliel has also been right, for Paul had indeed been found to be fighting against God (cf. 5:39).[3]

They had insisted from the outset that God had raised Jesus from the dead. Paul would eventually concur: "And if Christ has not been raised, our preaching is useless and so is your faith" (1 Cor. 15:14).

Gamaliel had also been right. This recalls a time when the apostles were brought before the Sanhedrin. "We gave you strict orders not to teach in this name," they were reminded. "You have filled Jerusalem with your teaching and are determined to make us guilty of this man's blood" (Acts 5:28).

"We must obey God rather than man!" the apostles exclaimed. "The God of our fathers raised Jesus from the dead—whom you had killed by hanging him on a tree.

God exalted him to his own right hand as Prince and Savior that he might give repentance and forgiveness of sins to Israel."

When they heard this, they were furious and wanted to put them to death. However, a Pharisee named *Gamaliel*—a rabbi honored by all the people, stood up and ordered that the apostles be put outside for a little while. Then he addressed the members of the Sanhedrin:

> Men of Israel, consider carefully what you intend to do to these men. Some time ago Theudas appeared, claiming to be somebody, and about four hundred men rallied to him. He was killed, all his followers were dispersed, and it all came to nothing. After him, Judas the Galilean . . . . Therefore, in the present case I advise you: Leave these men alone! Let them go! For if their purpose or activity is of human origin, it will fail. But if it is from God, you will not be able to stop these men, you will only find yourselves fighting against God.

While his reasoning prevailed, Paul was not convinced. Now he had cause to reconsider.

The men accompanying Paul stood by speechless. They appear to have heard the sound, but could not make out what was said. Paul got up to his feet, but had lost his sight. So they led him by the hand to Damascus. For three days he remained blind, and fasted for the interim.

Then he was visited by a disciple named *Ananias*. "Brother, Saul" he greeted him, "the Lord—Jesus, who appeared to you on the road as you were coming here—has sent me so that you may see again and be filled with the Holy Spirit." Immediately, Paul's sight was restored. He broke his fast, and regained his strength.

This was not the kind of experience one would likely forget. While as a rule referred to as his conversion experience, his calling as an apostle to the Gentiles seems more prominent. As Ananias was informed, "This man is my chosen instrument to carry my name before the Gentiles and their kings and before the people of Israel."

Paul maintained that a person was called *in Christ*. As a result, to negotiate life together—in keeping with the corporate character of the Christian faith. In this regard, to assume his or her own special place of service. However, this is a topic we shall explore more at length at a later point.

The apostle spent several days with the disciples in Damascus. He immediately took upon himself the imposing challenge of preaching the gospel in the synagogues, and those who heard him were astonished that someone who had been instrumental in persecuting the followers of Jesus was now championing the cause.

He became more *powerful and baffled* his opposition, while demonstrating that Jesus was the Christ—to the consternation of those who disagreed with him. Some conspired to kill him. He was able to escape with the help of other believers, and made his way up to Jerusalem. One can only imagine what thoughts raced through his mind as he retraced his footsteps.

Upon arriving at his destination, Paul attempted to join with the disciples. Nevertheless, they were afraid of him—recalling how he had vigorously persecuted the fellowship. Barnabas subsequently took the initiative, and brought him to the apostles. He informed them of Paul's transforming encounter with the risen Christ, and resulting ministry. Accordingly, he was accepted, and boldly preached *in the name of the Lord*.

Once again, there were some determined to kill him. When this became known, the *brothers* brought him to Caesarea and sent him off to Tarsus. Here he would meet with family and friends of long standing. It goes without saying that some would be more sympathetic to his transformation than others. In any case, Paul drops out of sight for the time being.

Now a great number of persons had turned to the Lord in Antioch. When news of this reached Jerusalem, Barnabas was sent to appraise the situation. He was encouraged by what he witnessed, and stayed on to minister to them. "He was a good man," Luke appreciatively observes, "full of the Holy Spirit and faith, and a great number of people were brought to the Lord" (11:24).

Whereupon, Barnabas went to Tarsus in search for Paul. When he had found him, he brought him back to Antioch. They labored there together for a whole year, instructing a great number of persons in the faith. It was in this context that the Christ of faith took on additional implications.

No two experiences are precisely the same, and some differ more than others. It came to pass that "Paul and his companions traveled throughout the region of Phrygia and Galatia, having been kept by the Holy Spirit from preaching the word in the province of Asia"(Acts 16:6). The apostle

> may have intended to make for Ephesus on the west coast of Asia, (but) this section makes it overwhelmingly clear that (his) progress was directed by God in a variety of ways, so that the missionaries were led into new areas of work. The whole account is related at breath-taking speed, to convey the impression of the irresistible sweep of events.[4]

They were permitted to minister extensively in the region of Phrygia and Galatia. Some would have settled for less, seeing that there always remains work to be done. Paul was not of that sort, but was intent on sowing the seed on virgin soil.

Furthermore, the Holy Spirit prohibited them from preaching the word in Asia for the time being. The opportunity would be afforded them later on. To allow for the obvious, timing can be a critical factor in any undertaking. Luke does not provide any detail, so that we are left to speculate.

They then attempted to enter Bithynia, but *the Spirit of Jesus* would not allow them to do so. Once again, Luke offers no explanation. However, we are left with the impression that there were urgent matters to be taken care of elsewhere. So they went down to Troas. There, during the night, Paul had a vision of a Macedonian man begging him: "Come over to Macedonia and help us." Paul and his companions immediately prepared to comply, supposing that God had summoned them to a new phase in their ministry.

As can readily be seen, God employs a variety of ways to make his will known. It is sometimes through circumstances. One door closes, while another opens. We attempt one thing, only to turn to another.

It is sometimes through the still, small voice of God. Something less than a whisper, and hardly discernable. Yet, this is as valid as if it were to come in some more extraordinary manner.

It can be through a vision (cf. 9:10, 12; 10:3, 17; 22:17). Not that we should suppose that this is the customary fashion, since there are complex factors involved. It remains for God to decide the means.

Since it is said that they determined the significance of the vision, it would appear that some deliberation went into the process. Consequently, reason may play a role in divine guidance. As an acquaintance observed, "Since God gave me a mind, I suppose he meant me to use it."

The counsel of others may be involved. Most of what we hold as true, we have derived from others. We normally turn to those who are well informed in their discipline for input. This is increasingly so with increased specialization.

Those involved have to make the final call. It is not a responsibility some other person can assume. Each person must give an account for his or her behavior. Then, too, God's justice is impeccable.

We can as a rule refine our understanding of God's leading. In the course of time, and a change in circumstances. Accordingly, procrastination is often the cause for failure. So things would seem to appear from a Pauline perspective.

We will consider one more example concerning the apostle's experience with the Christ of faith. "I know a man in Christ who fourteen years ago was caught up to the third heaven," Paul asserts. "He heard inexpressible things, things that man is not permitted to tell" (2 Cor. 12:2, 4). He is speaking concerning himself.

The first heaven likely consists of our immediate environment, and the second concerning the expanse above. Moreover, the third heaven exists outside our space/time continuum—as the place of God's eternal abode. Paul reports being caught up into this exalted realm.

There he heard things that were inexpressible. This, in turn, invites a brief aside into the range of literary genre extant in Holy Writ. *Wisdom literature* concerns that which can be readily discerned by the observant. "Go to the ant, you sluggard; consider its ways and be wise!" (Prov. 6:6). I can recall as a child bending low over an ant hill, watching the tiny creatures scurry back and forth. Even then I was impressed by their industry, and wondered how they coordinated their activity.

Conversely, *prophetic literature* employs propositional truth as a means of communication. Consequently, we are assured: "All Scripture is God-breathed and is useful for teaching, rebuking, correcting and training in righteousness, so that the man of God may be thoroughly equipped for every good work" (2 Tim. 3:16).

Finally, *apocalyptic literature* resembles word pictures. As such, not along the line of propositional truth. This brings us at least to the threshold of the inexpressible. Paul's experience is likely meant to reaffirm God's sovereign power and benevolent intent. Not unlike "a door standing open in heaven," and a voice inviting

John: "Come up here, and I will show you what must take place after this" (Rev. 4:1).

"To keep me from becoming conceited because of these surpassingly great revelations, there was given me a thorn in the flesh," he continues. "Three times I pleaded with the Lord to take it away from me. But he said to me, 'My grace is sufficient for you, for my power is made perfect in weakness!'" (2 Cor. 12:7-8).

The apostle's *thorn in the flesh* has given rise to expansive speculation. It has been variously identified as spiritual temptation, opposition and persecution, sexual temptation, physical appearance, epilepsy, migraine headaches, impaired eye-sight, and re-occurring malarial fever. In any case, a continued inhibition and frustration.

Three times is likely idiomatic, suggesting repeated petition. It was a matter of considerable concern, one that invited urgent supplication. Not simply for the sake of the supplicant, but that the work might continue uninhibited. Needless to say, there was much at stake with the apostle being able to effectively fulfill his critical calling.

Rather than being granted his request, Paul was assured that the Lord's grace was sufficient for any eventuality. *Grace* here is to be understood in terms of empowerment. Moreover, it is mediated through weakness, supposing that it leads one to rely on the spiritual resources available.

Several comments would seem in order. First, there is no simple correlation between piety and physical health. One who lives a godly life is more likely to enjoy robust health, but not necessarily so. Recall Job in this connection. In particular, it is said that the practice of prayer results not only in better health, but quicker recovery.

Second, "Jesus Christ is the same yesterday and today and forever" (Heb. 13:8). Changing circumstances notwithstanding. Not simply in good times, but in adverse circumstances.

Finally, in paradoxical fashion: "For when I am weak, then I am strong" (2 Cor. 12:10).

> In paganism, divine power was especially displayed in magical wonders; for Paul, it is God's power enabling one weak in himself to endure.... Although Paul had performed many miracles (12:12), he would not boast in his miracles, as his opponents perhaps boasted in theirs; instead he boasted in his weaknesses.[5]

Paul elsewhere confesses, "I have learned the secret of being content in any and every situation, whether fed or hungry, whether living in plenty or in want. I can do everything through him who gives me strength" (Phil. 4:12-13). This contentment appears to have been something that he acquired over the passing of time, and as a result of different circumstances.

Thus we are reminded of the sage counsel, "Trust in the Lord with all your heart and lean not on your own understanding; in all your ways acknowledge him, and he will make your paths straight" (Prov. 3:5-6). Then as elaborated in the so-called *Serenity Prayer* (attributed by some to Reinhold Niebuhr):

God grant me the serenity to accept the things I cannot change;
courage to change the things I can;
and wisdom to know the difference.

Living one day at a time;
Enjoying one moment at a time;
Accepting hardships as the pathway to peace;

Taking, as He did, this sinful world as it is , not as I would have it;
Trusting that He will make all things right if I surrender to His will;
That I may be reasonably happy in this life and supremely happy with Him
Forever in the next. Amen.

This seems quite in consort with the Pauline emphasis on the Christ of faith.

ONE AMONG MANY

As previously noted, Paul accents the personal dimension of life in Christ. It remains to explore what this may entail for any given individual, the apostle being singled out as a special instance. Consequently, the chapter title is meant to recall the observation that anyone with God is in the majority.

Strictly speaking, life begins at inception. If allowed to run its course, the fetus will be born a human. Well before that time, it is capable of survival. No two fetuses are precisely the same, and they increasingly differentiate—even while within their mothers' wombs.

One would hope that the child would be welcome. Not all are so fortunate. Qualifications aside, Hebrew children were considered a divine blessing. Consequently, we may assume that Paul was among the more advantaged.

According to Jewish tradition, three are implicated in the birth of a child. Its parents and the Almighty. All three are said to have invested interests, but God's investment ought to be paramount. Parents alike defer to God, out of reverence and concern for the child's welfare.

One might name the child for a variety of reasons. It was often derived from a family member. Sometimes it recalled a memorable event, which demonstrated God's faithfulness. Sometimes it expressed a goal toward which the child might aspire. In any case, to differentiate the child from others.

They called him *Saul*, likely after the first of Israel's rulers. He was from the tribe of Benjamin, as was his name's sake. The name meant *asked*, with the implication of *asked of God*. He also received as a Roman cognomen the alternative *Paul*.

The apostle assures us that he grew up in a traditional Jewish home. One where faith is sensed before being articulated. Where the father appears as a benevolent authority figure, accountable to the Almighty. Where the mother uniquely reflects God's mercy and compassion. For all practical purposes, where the home resembles an extension of the holy land.

Paul was differentiated from the idolatry-prone Gentiles. Idolatry was identified as the chief culprit in man's defection, since it failed to render the honor due the

Almighty, and perverted life in general.

There was, however, a counterpoint. It was said that God loves a righteous Gentile more than the High Priest (per se). I take it that this observation should be understood in the context that more is expected of those to whom more is given. In other words, with privilege comes commensurate responsibility.

"Remember the Sabbath day by keeping it holy," the Israelites were enjoined. "Six days you shall labor and do all your work, but the seventh day is a Sabbath to the Lord your God" (Exod. 20:9-10). It became customary to count toward the Sabbath: first day, second day, and the like. In this manner, building toward a climax.

The rabbis speculated that persons were given an *additional soul*, "enabling them to experience a 'double' measure and spirituality. The weekly Sabbath uplifts the spirit of the tormented Jew and enables him to transcend his life of drudgery and to feel physically and spiritually refreshed, able to confront another week."[1] One's potential was thus enhanced and his or her horizon broadened.

The Jewish calendar is punctuated with religious holidays. The major festivals fall into two categories: the Pilgrim Holy Days of Passover, Pentecost, and Tabernacles—when Jews of ancient times would make a special effort to worship in the temple precinct, and the High Holy Days comprising Rosh Hashanah and Yom Kippur. The minor festivals embrace Purim and Hanukkah. Shivah Asar b'Tammus and Tisha b'Av constitute prominent fast days.

Passover commemorates the seminal event in the history of the Jewish people: their deliverance from bondage. They were instructed to sprinkle the blood of a lamb on the doorposts of their homes, so that the angel of death would pass them by. A ritual meal was observed on that occasion.

The term *seder* means an order of service. In this connection, Paul would have been encouraged to recognize the link between slavery and deliverance, our adversity and joy. As for commentary:

> We are neither to be fixated and obsessed with past suffering nor overly and unrealistically optimistic about the future.... Passover bids us to remember the good and bad, our joys and our tribulations, our past suffering and our hopes for the world's future redemption.[2]

Pentecost gets its name from being celebrated the fiftieth day after Passover. It was originally a harvest festival. Consequently, it was a time for celebrating the Lord's provision. In lean years, since they had survived the ordeal. In good years, because they enjoyed abundance, which would allow them to lay by for less fortunate occasions.

With the passing of time and circumstances, the festival increasingly became associated with the giving of the covenant. The first reading concerns the glory of the Lord. The second is an encouragement to persist in faith.

The Feast of Sukkoth (Tabernacles) comes in the fall, four days after Yom Kippur. It solicits rejoicing, in sharp contrast to the somber, introspective observance that precedes it. On that occasion, devout Jews give thanks for their "redemption from Egypt and for God's providence during the many years of wandering through the desert. By dwelling in an exposed, insecure hut, we are reminded that true security comes from being sheltered under God's protective wings."[3]

The festival also assumed a messianic orientation. This, in turn, implicated the Gentiles. As an example, Jews are reminded that no one is genuinely free while anyone remains in slavery.

The High Holy Days begin in the fall with Rosh Hashanah—the Jewish new year, and conclude ten days later with Yom Kippur—the Day of Atonement. The preceding month of Elul is set aside for reflection and soul-searching, and has come to be known as *the days of awe*.

According to tradition, it is on Rosh Hashanah that God decides who will live and die during the succeeding year. Along a related line, it is said that God heals us from every illness but the last. All things considered, persons were to seize the opportunities that life affords them.

The *akeda* (binding of Isaac, cf. Gen. 22) is read on this occasion. It serves to recall Abraham's obedient trust and resilient faith. It no less accents God's faithful provision.

Yom Kippur provides the culmination to the High Holy Day's redemptive drama. It is accompanied by fasting, prayer, and introspection. Fasting is not viewed as an end in itself, but a means to an end. In particular, so as to prod persons to realize their spiritual obligations.

Repentance is stressed throughout the High Holy Days. It constitutes a turning away from sin, and turning to God. Thus are we assured that there is no freedom *from* that does not involve freedom *for*. This was evidenced by the Israelites covenanting with God after their deliverance from bondage.

I will touch on the Minor Holidays only in passing. Purim recalls the time when Esther interceded for her people, threatened with annihilation. It is the occasion of unbridled joy. It provides and opportunity for giving gifts, and exuberant behavior.

Hanukkah (Feast of Dedication) commemorates the victory of the Maccabees over Antiochus Epiphanies. The latter had attempted to impose Hellenism on a reluctant subject people. The festival marks the victory of the few over the many, the weak over the mighty, those who choose freedom over the dreaded tyrants of the world.

The most solemn occasion in the Jewish year falls in the summertime, when the destruction of the temple and exile are recalled for posterity. Shivah Asar b'Tammuz commemorates the first breach of the Jerusalem walls by the invading Babylonians. It also serves to recall the halting of the daily temple sacrifices, the burning of the Torah scrolls, and the erection of idols in the temple precinct during the Roman incursion. It is likewise said to be on the day Moses broke the first set of tablets.

The fast of Tisha b'Av culminates a three-week period of mourning. Although it, too, marks a number of tragedies, it primarily recalls the fatal coincidence of the destruction of the two Jerusalem temples. Before that, the failure of the people to enter the promised land.

Now while the celebration of the Jewish liturgical year was still in the process of refinement, Paul's life was oriented toward such ritual observances. This involved both what he shared with others of like persuasion, and associated remembrances—as would be expected of anyone raised as a son of the covenant.

Paul was circumcised in keeping with God's injunction to Abraham (cf. Gen. 17:12). Circumcision does not make a person Jewish, but recognizes his Jewishness. It serves as a constant reminder of one's obligation for observing the covenant. One who was willfully disobedient was depicted as *uncircumcised in heart* (cf. Acts 7:51).

The practice of *bar/bat mitzvah*, meaning *son/daughter of the commandments*, dates from recent times. It, nevertheless, reflects the established conviction that children would at an appropriate age assume their covenant responsibilities.

Marriage was considered a sacred institution. "For this reason a man will leave his father and mother and be united to his wife, and they will become one flesh" (Gen. 2:24). *Leave his father and mother* must be understood in a relative sense, since Israelite marriage was as a rule patrilocal—taking up residence in or near the father's residence.

They will become one flesh.

This does not denote merely the sexual union that follows marriage, or the children conceived in marriage, or even the spiritual and emotional relationship that it involves, though all are involved in becoming one flesh. Rather it affirms that just as blood relations are one's flesh and bone, so marriage creates a similar kinship relation between man and wife.[4]

It comes as no surprise that marriage was held in high esteem among the Jewish people. Those who refrained were thought to have violated the *mitzvah* (commandment, good work) of procreation. Then, too, they had forfeited the opportunity for a mutually beneficial relationship.

Paul, however, opted not to marry. "Don't we have the right to take a believing wife along with us," he rhetorically inquires, "as do the other apostles and the Lord's brothers and Cephus?" (1 Cor. 9:5). Even so, he points out that an unmarried man can give his full attention to the proclamation of the gospel (cf. 1 Cor. 7:32). Needless to add, the exception does not prove the rule.

It comes time to let the apostle speak for himself. "If anyone else thinks he has reasons to put confidence in the flesh," he invites a comparison, "I have more: circumcised on the eighth day, of the people of Israel, of the tribe of Benjamin, a Hebrew of Hebrews; in regard to the law, a Pharisee; as for zeal, persecuting the church; as for legalistic righteousness, faultless" (Phil. 3:4-6). *Of the people of Israel* may mean to set him off from the proselytes, who were to some degree treated as second-rate citizens.

A Hebrew of Hebrews reflects

the Hebrew-Hellenistic distinction (cf. Acts 6:1). "Hellenistic Judaism" normally designates Jews of the Dispersion who adopted Greek as their language and whose way of life reflected their non-Jewish surroundings. This generalization can be very misleading, because many Hellenistic Jews were distinguished by their orthodoxy (while numerous Palestinian Jews were throughly Hellenized). Having been born and reared in Tarsus, however, Paul might have been suspect in this regard, and so here he makes it clear that his family upbringing was irreproachable.[5]

Even so, Hellenistic influence is evidenced in his literary expression. As for commentary:

> Even though he uses a variety of Greek anthropological terms to explain aspects of human behavior in sections of his letters, he often does so on an *ad hoc* basis with the result that there is little overall consistency evident.... Paul was an eclectic who drew upon a variety of anthropological conceptions in a manner subsidiary or tangential to the more immediate concerns he addresses in his extant letters.[6]

In regard to the law, a Pharisee. The term *Pharisee* is derived from the notion of separation, first from the influences of Hellenism and eventually from any who would disagree. "Now, for the Pharisees," Josephus appreciatively elaborates, "they live meanly, and despise delicacies in diet; and they follow the conduct of reason; and what that prescribes to them as good for them, they do; and they think they ought earnestly to strive to serve reason's dictates for practice."[7]

They were also respectful concerning the elderly, in keeping with their high regard for tradition. While holding that God is sovereign, they supposed that persons were allowed to choose between walking his ways and disregarding them. They anticipated a future life, wherein the righteous would be rewarded and the wicked punished. All things considered, the populace characteristically held them in high esteem.

As for zeal, persecuting the church. Zeal is usually thought of as a virtue. In this regard, my mother would caution: "Anything that is worth doing is worth doing well." However, zeal can be misappropriated. "I can testify about them that they are zealous," Paul says concerning his fellow Jews, "but their zeal is not based on knowledge" (Rom. 10:2).

The apostle would subsequently turn his zeal toward advancing the great commission. "For I am the least of apostles and do not even deserve to be called an apostle, because I persecuted the church of God," Paul concludes. "But by the grace of God I am what I am, and his grace to me was not without effect. No, I worked harder than all of them—yet not I, but the grace of God that was with me" (1 Cor. 15:9-10).

As for legal righteousness, faultless. "Under Gamaliel I was thoroughly trained in the law of our fathers and was just as zealous for God as any of you are today," the apostle confidently affirmed (Acts 22:3). Then, at a later point, he testified: "So

I strive to keep my conscience clear before God and man" (Acts 24:16).

There was, nonetheless, a downside. "For what I want to do I do not do, but what I hate I do," Paul agonizingly confessed. "For in my inner being I delight in God's law, but I see another law at work in the members of my body, waging war against the law of my mind and making me a prisoner of the law of sin at work within my members" (Rom. 7:15, 22).

As for apt commentary,

> When one discovers not only a power at work within oneself against one's best desires, but also a powerlessness to combat it, then one must look for help beyond oneself. Paul is not in the market for a self-help program. He is not hoping for a lucky break or turning over a new leaf. He is a drowning man crying out for **rescue!**[8]

A person plays many roles in a lifetime, and Paul proves to be no exception. Some come about in the course of events, while others are acquired. Paul was a male, which would normally associate him with his father in an apprentice role. Even rabbis were encouraged to have a trade.

When the apostle arrived at Corinth, he stayed with Aquila and Priscilla and worked with them, since he was also a tentmaker (cf. Acts 18:3). The term was apparently "applied to leather working in general. As a leather worker, Paul would have been an artisan. Artisans were typically proud of their work, despite the long hours they had to invest to succeed, and were higher than peasants in status and income."[9]

As previously noted, he was nurtured in the law by Gamaliel. He, in turn, was associated with the School of Hillel. More permissive than the rival school of Shammai, it proved to be more influential.

In his rabbinical role, Paul was essentially a teacher. While not required to lead public worship, he might be called upon to deliver a homily. This was in keeping with the recognition of his advanced study. It was preferred that those invited to speak were able to articulate well. The apostle met both criteria.

Paul was also a Roman citizen. "Is it legal for you to flog a Roman citizen who hasn't even been found guilty?" he protested (Acts 22:25).

This sent the centurion off to report the matter to his commander. "What are you going to do?" he asked. "This man is a Roman citizen."

The commander hastened to explore the matter with his prisoner. "Tell me," he demanded, "are you a Roman citizen?"

"Yes, I am," Paul replied.

The commander observed, "I had to pay a big price for my citizenship." The practice was officially discouraged.

"But I was born a citizen," the apostle responded. While Luke does not detail how this came about, he leaves no doubt but that it was considered a great privilege. Of course, with the privilege comes a commensurate responsibility. In particular, making every reasonable effort to maintain the *Pax Romana*.

Paul is best remembered in his role as an apostle. An apostle is one sent on behalf of another. Consequently, the one who is sent is to be received as the one who sends him.

Paul appears to have taken readily to the mentor role implied in his apostolic calling. He warned Timothy concerning false teachers, who advocate ascetic practices—which have the effect of denying the goodness of God's creation. "If you point these things out to the brothers, you will be a good minister of Christ Jesus, brought up in the truths of the faith and of the good teaching that you have followed," he subsequently admonishes (1 Tim. 4:6).

"Don't let anyone look down on you because you are young," he shortly adds, "but set an example for the believers in speech, in life, in love, in faith and in purity" (v. 12). *In speech*, since a tree is known by the fruit it bears. *In life*, because we resemble living epistles—known and read by all. *In love*, which reflects God's compassion for his wayward creatures. *In faith*, as those who trust God's promises. *In purity*, not compromised by the ways of the world.

The time would come when Paul was called upon to play the martyr. "For I am already being poured out like a drink offering, and the time has come for my departure," he recognizes.

> I have fought the good fight, I have finished the race, I have kept the faith. Now there is in store for me the crown of righteousness, which the Lord, the righteous judge, will award to me on that day—and not only to me, but also to all who have longed for his appearing (2 Tim. 4:6-8).

The initial metaphors suggest that the apostle was of the opinion that the time of his demise was fast approaching. *Being poured out* implies a libation (cf. Num. 15:5, 7, 10), as if a sacrifice well-pleasing to the Lord. *Departure* conveys images of breaking camp to begin a new journey, or leaving port for a distant destination. Coupled together, they imply transition.

I have fought the good fight. "For our struggle is not against flesh and blood," Paul observes elsewhere, "but against the rulers, against the authorities, against the powers of this dark world and against the spiritual forces of evil in the heavenly realms" (Eph. 6:12). It is not necessary to assume that all authorities were antagonistic to the gospel, although many were. Then, too, the evil prince of this world appears capable of turning even good intention into adverse circumstances.

"Therefore," the apostle admonishes, "put on the whole armor of God, so that when the day of evil comes, you may be able to stand your ground, and after you have done everything, to stand." Since the believer is adequately equipped to contend with the foe. Paul speaks from experience.

I have finished the course. The apostle does not say that he has won the race, although this ought to be one's intent (cf. 1 Cor. 9:24). Get a good start, maintain a consistent pace, and finish strong. Do not be distracted by unrelated concerns.

Not all are equally endowed. No matter, since the important thing is to be a good steward. In this regard, the apostle serves as a prime example for others to emulate.

I have kept the faith. Perhaps in the sense of having run according the course laid out. Not straying from the way, nor improvising. Whereupon, to hear the commendation: "Well done, good and faithful servant! You have been faithful with a few things; I will put you in charge of many things. Come and share your master's happiness" (Matt. 25:23).

The Christian martyr was sometimes criticized for his or her show of emotion at the time of demise. Life was too precious a commodity to surrender in stoic fashion. Still, the martyr would not compromise his or her faith to prolong temporal life at the expense of eternity.

All things considered, Paul was said to have been "a man small in size, bald-headed, bandy-legged, well-built, with eyebrows meeting, rather long-nosed, full of grace. For sometimes he seemed like a man, and sometimes he had the countenance of an angel."[10] Despite all the disparity in his appearance, he eminently qualified as a majority of one.

A CORPORATE IDENTITY

Life originates from an intimate social relationship. It would not persist were it not for the caring concern of others. Except on exceedingly rare occasions, it continues to be nurtured in a supportive social context. All thing considered, this gives rise to the concept of *a minority of one*.

"A woman giving birth to a child has pain because her time has come," Jesus observed; "but when her baby is born she forgets the anguish because of her joy that a child is born into the world" (John 16:21). In a characteristic manner, suitable for proverbial purposes.

The birthed child grasps for life. It has been exposed to a strange and threatening environment. As noted above, it would not long survive without assistance. Its mother is as a rule the primary care-giver. Breast-feeding provides an intimate and satisfactory means.

The infant is scarcely aware of what is going on around it. Ill-defined images come and go. Sounds rumble to and fro. One thing is certain, it is not alone but associated with others.

It becomes increasingly aware of the parameters of the self. What is mine and that which belongs to another individual. My toe, although it has not learned the nomenclature. Your hand, since it is manipulated by someone else.

It soon learns that crying is an effective means of getting attention. It cannot as yet articulate its wants. Someone else must appraise the situation. While the system leaves much to be desired, it will have to do for the present. Moreover, it does not know what the future holds in store.

The infant becomes more perceptive as time goes on. It can differentiate between its parents. If there are siblings, they too must be singled out. These significant others seem more or less receptive. On some occasions more than on others.

Additional persons impinge on the child's life. Relatives of various sorts: uncles, aunts, cousins, and the like. There are also friends of the family, and more casual acquaintances.

Social configurations begin to emerge.

About ten thousand years ago, man learned how to produce food by domesticating certain plants and animals. This development, whose importance for human history cannot be overemphasized, took place in the ancient Near East and led to the establishment of the oldest villages in the world inhabited by farming people.[1]

The typical Near Eastern village consists of a tightly packed cluster of houses, with winding narrow alleys, bounded by farm lands. It was constructed to fulfill three essential needs: security against the forces of nature and the incursion of hostile people, an ample water supply, and fertile soil. Life was precarious under the best of conditions, and conditions seldom approached the ideal.

The physical appearances of the village depended in substantial measure on the building materials available. In a mountain region, it might consist largely of stone. If on a plain, then likely from mud-dried bricks. The buildings ranged from simple one-room structures to complex multi-room enclosures. Extended families often inhabited a compound within the village. This consisted of several adjoining houses, all opening onto one courtyard—with a gate leading out into the street.

The village was essentially self-sufficient. The local potter crafted vessels from clay. The carpenter made plows, beams, and such. Persons as a rule received pay in kind. In any case, village life was wed to the land. As a result, the inhabitants were derided by the Bedouin as *slaves of the soil*.

Most males enjoyed relatively slack seasons, alternating with periods of intensive work in the fields. "Not so the women, whose routine consists of daily repetition of the same chores: fetching water, grinding corn, baking bread, preparing meals, kneading the dung for fuel, taking care of the children, spinning, weaving, embroidering, and so forth."[2]

The staple diet consisted largely of cereals and legumes, vegetables less often, still less fish and animal products. The exception was on festive occasions. For instance, the elder brother complained:

> Look! All these years I've been slaving for you and never disobeyed your orders. Yet you never gave me even a young goat so I could celebrate with my friends. But when this son of yours who has squandered your property with prostitutes comes home, you kill the fattened calf for him! (Luke 15:29-30).

The kinship structure provided the basis for settling disputes, either on its own or in conjunction with the village elders. More serious disagreements called for more formal arbitration. Decisions were thought binding.

For all practical purposes, hospitality was considered a sacred obligation. It was no less deemed a privilege. It served the need for security and sustenance. It was, however, not to be abused.

Paul was well acquainted with village culture, even though he was raised in Tarsus, which he appreciatively characterizes as "no ordinary city" (Acts 22:39). He was was subsequently educated in Jerusalem. It goes without saying that urban life at the time differs considerably from today. Even so, life was modified from the virtually pervasive village culture.

As an example, there was a proliferation of trades and crafts. An urbanite might own land and make a living from income derived from the land, without being personally engaged in agriculture. He might even choose to move to a village, and spend his life there—without actually adapting to the village lifestyle.

Social status became more pronounced in an urban setting. The more affluent indulged themselves, not uncommonly at the expense of those less fortunate. Marriage became more restricted, involving those of similar social cast. Justice often suffered as a result of privilege.

Walter Brueggemann distinguishes between *shalom* (peace, well-being) for the have-nots and haves. As for the former, "People who live in the midst of precariousness shape their vocabulary and their faith, their perceptions and their liturgy in a distinctive way. One of the most important ways the Israelites expressed their faith was around the them of 'cry out, hear, and deliver.'"[3] In distress, they call out to the Lord for deliverance. Whereupon, he hears their petition and sets out to deliver them.

As for the latter,

> It is the well-off who can reflect on proper management, who are aware that blessings have been given to them that must be wisely cared for and properly maintained for the generations to come. It is the well-off who can be reflective enough to care intentionally about the joyous celebration of life.[4]

Moreover, it is for the well-off to use their material resources wisely so as to address the social problems that persist.

Paul could appreciate *shalom* from both perspectives. Since he was from an artisan social cast, he had life better than most. Still, there were occasions when he was hard pressed to make ends meet, such as when he moved in with Aquila and Priscilla—working at their common trade (cf. 1 Cor. 18:2-3). Until, that is, he was joined by Silas and Timothy, presumably bringing with them support from the established churches.

Urban areas were decidedly more cosmopolitan, and Jews were singled out for mention (cf. Acts 15:21). As noted previously, they were tempted to assimilate. Paul's family was disposed to maintain their religious and ethnic distinctive, even though they were not allowed to do so in social isolation.

While urban life might be discussed at considerable length, I will touch on only a few additional features. First, persons were relatively anonymous. Unlike village life, where everyone more or less knows everyone else. The latter has been graphically described as living in a fishbowl.

Along a related line, one has more casual acquaintances. Even so, these relationships can be rewarding. Then, too, the social matrix allows persons a greater degree of freedom to select individuals for more in-depth relationships. This is often with less corresponding demands than associated with village life.

Persons are also more mobile. They as a rule travel further from home, and stay for longer periods of time. This permits them a larger range of experience, and fosters a cosmopolitan attitude.

Perhaps I have pursued the present line of thinking far enough to illustrate the social milieu of the apostle Paul. It consisted of a virtually pervasive village mentality, as qualified by an urban setting. Tarsus at first, Jerusalem at a later juncture, and then by way of the Mediterranean world of his day.

The topic, however, can readily be expanded regarding what Dietrich Bonhoeffer identifies as *mandates*. "The Scriptures name four such mandates: labor, marriage (and the family), government, and the Church. We speak of divine mandates rather than of divine orders because the word mandate refers more closely to a divinely imposed task."[5] So as to place the emphasis on our responsibility in these select areas, rather than the institutional order they come to assume.

Labor. The mandate of labor confronts us early on in the biblical narrative. It is written, "The Lord God took the man and put him in the Garden of Eden to work it and take care of it" (Gen. 2:18). We are thus assured that labor is both natural and desirable. After the fall, it serves as a means of discipline and grace.

Two enduring images occur to me concerning humans. First, concerning someone in prayer. A person's failure to pray is not only reprehensible but unnatural. It resembles a fish out of water.

Second, someone at work. Engaged in some worthwhile enterprise. Such as the potter at his wheel, or the harvester gathering grain. Each as appropriate to his or her particular calling.

One image might subsequently be imposed on the other. At worship and at work, and not one to the exclusion of the other. Accordingly, the rabbis reasoned that it was necessary to diligently perform labor on six days in order to genuinely observe the seventh—since they are inexorably linked together.

Industry must be coupled with generosity. For instance, Jesus told a parable concerning a rich man who enjoyed a bumper crop. "What shall I do?" he thought to himself. "I have no place to store my crops" (Luke 12:17). It apparently did not occur to him that he might share with those less fortunate.

"I will tear down my barns and build bigger ones, and there I will store all my grain and my goods," he concluded. "And I'll say to myself, 'You have plenty of good things laid up for many years. Take life easy; eat, drink and be merry.'" Again, without thought for the needs of others.

"You fool!" God reprimanded him. "This very night your life will be demanded from you. Then who will get what you have prepared for yourself?" *Yourself* reveals the focus of his attention. Lacking generosity, he failed to carry through with the mandate concerning labor, thus incurring God's rebuke.

Marriage and the family. "It is not good for man to dwell alone," God concluded early on. "I will make a helper suitable for him" (Gen. 2:18). We are thereby alerted to a beneficial character of the marital relationship.

"For this reason a man will leave his father and mother and be united to his wife, and they will become one flesh," the text continues. So as to bond together, for mutual benefit. In a perpetual union, before God and others.

"Wives," Paul singles out the wife, "submit to your husbands as to the Lord"

(Eph. 5:22). This is an extension of the injunction that submission is required of all. In other words, we are to defer to the concerns of others, rather than simply bent on furthering our own interests. The exhortation is now repeated in context of the marriage setting, as especially appropriate for the wife.

She is not meant to serve as a proverbial doormat: someone who uncritically embraces every whim of her partner. This would be in violation of the qualification *as to the Lord*, which implies a responsibility to live in accordance with Jesus' teaching and the dictates of conscience.

There may be sexual overtones to the injunction, although this would apply to both husband and wife. "Do not deprive one another except by mutual consent and for a time," the apostle enjoins elsewhere, "so that you may devote yourselves to prayer. Then come together again so that Satan will not tempt you because of your lack of self-control" (1 Cor. 7:5).

Otherwise, we ought to take it in a more general sense. Not in the sense of being demeaning but as an incentive to be gracious. Whereupon, not in strident fashion, as if to discredit her spouse. Consequently, seeking the welfare of all who are in some way implicated in the interplay of roles.

"Husbands, love your wives," the apostle continues, "Just as Christ loved the church and gave himself up for her to make her holy, cleansing her by the washing with water through the word" (Eph. 5:25). Love sacrificially, putting aside one's personal concerns so as to benefit one's spouse. So it can be readily seen that the husband's role is not less demanding or depreciating.

"Children, obey your parents in the Lord, for this is right," Paul adds. "'Honor your father and mother'—which is the first commandment with a promise—'that it may go well with you and that you may enjoy long life on the earth'" (cf. Exod. 20:12). *Obey your parents* since God wills it, and thus holds great promise. It should be noted that in this regard that families constitute the bedrock of society. Consequently, their erosion constitutes a dire threat for future generations.

"Listen my son, to your father's instruction and do not forsake your mother's teaching," the sage solemnly enjoins. "They will be a garland to grace your head and a chain to adorn your neck" (Prov. 1:8-9). Here parental instruction is set over against the enticement of sinners, the former as a paragon of virtue.

Incidently, Jewish tradition urges children heed their parents even if the latter are ill-tempered. In doing so, they may encourage their parents to mend their ways. Even if not, they have set the example for their own children to emulate.

Government.

> The divine mandate of government presupposes the divine mandates of labor and marriage. In the world which it rules, the governing authority finds already present the two mandates through which God the Creator exercises his creative power, and is therefore dependent. Government cannot itself produce life or values.[6]

Thus are governing authorities warned against usurping the prerogatives of parents, or inhibiting gainful activity. Only in extreme cases, where the health of children is genuinely at risk or labor practices may be injurious, and then so as to preserve the essential structure of these enterprises.

"Everyone must submit himself to the governing authorities, for there is no authority except that which God has established," Paul observes. "For rulers hold no terror for those who do right, but for those who do wrong" (Rom. 13:1, 4). In ideal terms, since the apostle makes no effort to describe an alternative course of action where government fails in its mission.

The church. Bonhoeffer reasons that the mandate concerning the church is in a qualified sense obligatory on all. In the sense that society is to respect the integrity of the Christian fellowship, and allowing it the opportunity to carry on its mission without restraint or disrespect. Conversely, not compromising its stand as a matter of political expediency or for some other reason.

In a more restricted sense, the mandate is addressed solely to church adherents. Then as both an individual obligation and corporate endeavor. This is said to be expressed in four regards. First, as expressive of its apostolic character. As concerns the early Christians, it was to their credit that they "devoted themselves to the apostles' doctrine and to the fellowship, to the breaking of bread and to prayer" (Acts 2:42).

For all practical purposes, we may say that the apostles' teaching came to be embodied in the New Testament. Since it appears that these texts originated with the apostles or those associated with them in their several missions. In contrast to the apocryphal writings that soon made their appearance, requiring an approved canon be formally recognized.

Second, in keeping with their unity in Christ. "For we are baptized by one Spirit into one body—whether Jews or Greeks, slave or free—and we are all given one Spirit to drink" (1 Cor. 12:13). As for commentary,

> The Spirit is what essentially distinguishes the believer from the nonbeliever (2:10-14); the Spirit is what especially marks the beginning of the Christian life (Gal. 3:2-3); the Spirit above all is what makes a person a child of God (Rom. 8:14-17). Thus it is natural for him to refer to their unity in the body in terms of the Spirit.[7]

It bears repeating, unity more resembles constructive diversity than stifling uniformity. Where even differences of opinion can reflect important nuances. Then, too, where various gifts can be beneficially exercised.

Third, so as to emulate God through holiness (cf. Lev. 19:2). In ritual terms, by constructing places of worship. Then by attending them faithfully, and enthusiastically participating in worship. In this connection, "Let us not give up meeting together, as some are in the habit of doing, and let us encourage one another—and all the more as you see the Day approaching" (Heb. 10:25).

In moral terms, by fostering piety. Along this line, "Make every effort to live in peace with all man and be holy; without holiness no one will see the Lord" (Heb. 12:14). Not in the sense of suppressing cherished convictions, but treating differences amicably. In the pursuit of holiness, and without exception or procrastination.

Finally, by way of realizing the universality (catholicity) of the Christian faith. In this connection, Helmut Thieleke recalls:

> Once, kneeling in the prairie sand of South-West Africa, I celebrated the Lord's Supper with some Hereto tribesmen. They had never heard of our city, and I had known nothing of that remote bush country.... Neither of us understood a single word of the other's language. But when I made the sign of the cross with my hand and pronounced the name "Jesus" their dark faces lit up. We ate the same bread and drank from the same chalice, despite apartheid, and they couldn't do enough to show me their love.[8]

I experienced something similar. I had been asked to participate in an ordination service. At one point the candidate knelt down, and we placed our hands on his head. As I gazed down, I was struck by the fact that there was one relatively large white hand (my own) partially obscured by several smaller black hands. I keenly sensed at that moment what Billy Graham describes as becoming *a world Christian*.

Our attention is called in conclusion to a poignant passage from Acts: "For two whole years Paul stayed there (in Rome) in his own rented house and welcomed all who came to see him. Boldly and without hindrance he preached the kingdom of God and taught about the Lord Jesus Christ" (28:30-31).

No reference is made concerning the source of his income. As mentioned earlier, he came from a family with some means. Moreover, he enjoyed the support of fellow believers. In turn, this brings to mind Jesus' teaching: "It is more blessed to give than to receive" (Acts 20:35).

Marriage and family is implicit in the social structure. We can readily imagine the apostle welcoming both husbands and their spouses in the course of time. Moreover, as he gave instruction concerning family affairs, and the roles persons fulfill in that regard. Husbands and wives, parents and children, and siblings.

Paul is quartered at the discretion of the governing authorities. There he awaits the impending hearing before Caesar, to whom he has appealed in keeping with his Roman citizenship. Since Luke offers no explanation concerning the extended detention, we can only speculate. It was perhaps a sensitive issue that the authorities hoped to defuse by not issuing too hasty a decision. Even then, they seem to have had second thoughts after the verdict was reached.

Conversely, the apostle seized the opportunity to boldly proclaim the gospel to any who would listen. It amounted to a cosmopolitan pulpit, from which he could minister to diverse people.

The details of his message can be readily reconstructed from his extensive correspondence. While he touched on all four mandates mentioned above, he especially focused on the church. In this manner, accenting its proper place in society. In addition, stressing its apostolic character—as foundational for its unity, holiness, and universality. Thus the apostle assumed his role within the Christian fellowship and society at large.

IN SITU

Humans exist within a space/time continuum. Their perspective is conditioned by their respective locations, as we shall see in the next two chapters. In particular, Paul's exposure to Christ originated in and was cultivated by his experience within the Mediterranean world of his day. *In situ* is derived from the Latin, meaning *in the original position*.

It begins with Tarsus, a city on the Cicilian plain, "watered by the Cnydus, and some 16 kilometers inland after the fashion of most cities on the Asia Minor coast. To judge from the extent of its remains, Tarsus must have housed a population of no less that half a million in Roman times."[1] As noted earlier, it was *no ordinary city*, hence worthy of note.

Tarsus appears to have been the scene of an extended struggle among competing ethnic groups. Consequently, Paul would have been raised in a highly cosmopolitan environ, which fostered a determination to maintain his Jewish tradition. This combination of factors would contribute to God's purpose that he serve as an apostle to the Gentiles.

The youth likely took leave for Jerusalem no earlier than his thirteenth birthday. It must have been with great anticipation that he set out for *The City of the Great King*. The psalmist speaks in glowing terms: "He has set his foundation on the holy mountain; the Lord loves the gates of Zion more that the dwellings of Jacob. Glorious things are said of you, O city of God" (87:1-3). In terms of pilgrimage, one always ascends to Jerusalem.

The ancient city was located on a spur, surrounded by deep ravines—except to the north. This aided in its defense against hostile intruders. The Gihon Spring provided a constant water supply before the population became too extensive, and additional sources were required.

By Paul's time, the city probably had a population of well over 400,000. Its viability was preeminently due to the extensive ritual services carried on within its precincts. Some lived in exceedingly lavish quarters, while others appear to have scarcely managed. This heightened the contrast between the affluent and the less fortunate populace.

According to Jewish tradition, if one wanted to get rich, he should go north to the Galilee. Here fertile soil awaited him, and commerce was prevalent. Conversely, if one wanted to become wise, he was encouraged to go south to Judea and Jerusalem in particular. Here the rabbis gathered their disciples around them to explore a common tradition, in the light of subsequent developments. Paul opted to join this select group.

It appears that he never personally encountered Jesus during the latter's earthly life and ministry. This is not surprising, since the base of Jesus' movement was the Galilee. He seldom traveled to Jerusalem, and then only during the heavy influx of pilgrims associated with the high festivals. Moreover, a crucifixion was not an uncommon event, even though his had higher visibility than most.

Nevertheless, the youthful rabbinic student would soon meet up with Jesus' followers—most notably Stephen. "Now, Stephen, a man full of God's grace and power, did great wonders and miraculous signs among the people. Opposition arose, however, from members of the Synagogue of the Freedmen" (Acts 6:8-9). *Freedmen* were former slaves or their children who were emancipated by their owners.

Unable to thwart Stephen's compelling reasoning, the opposition persuaded false witnesses to charge him with blasphemy. Taken before the Sanhedrin, he made a spirited defense. "You stiff-necked people," he charged them, "with uncircumcised hearts and ears! You are just like your fathers."

Upon hearing this accusation, they were furious, covered their ears, and while shouting at the top of their voices dragged him outside the city and began to stone him. Meanwhile, the witnesses laid their clothes at the feet of Paul, who was giving his approval to the death of the martyr.

On that day a great persecution broke out, and all but the apostles were scattered throughout Judea and Samaria. In context, it would appear that the persecution was aimed primarily at the Hellenists among the believers, although others were no doubt implicated. In any case, it would serve God's purpose to spread the good news into the surrounding regions.

Paul now sets out to bury the church along with Stephen. "Going from house to house, he dragged off men and women and put them in prison" (8:3).

> Drastic action was called for: these people, he thought, were not merely misguided enthusiasts who since embracing of error called for patient enlightenment; they were deliberate impostors, proclaiming that God has raised from the tomb to be Lord and Messiah a man whose manner of death was sufficient to show that the divine course rested on him.[2]

Not content, he sought authorization from the high priest to carry his crusade to the synagogues located in Damascus. Damascus was the chief city of Syria. It was strategically located east of the Anti-Lebanon Mountains, within sight of Mount Hermon to the southwest. As noted earlier, it was as he was approaching his destination that he encountered the risen Lord, and the zealous persecutor was transformed into an equally zealous missionary. In retrospect, one would not imagine Paul being half-hearted about any enterprise.

There was in the church of Syrian Antioch a number of prophets and teachers, seemingly drawn from a broad range of ethnic and social backgrounds. Antioch was located on the Orontes, some 500 kilometers north of Jerusalem. "Even under the Seleucids the inhabitants had gained a reputation for energy, insolence and instability, which manifested itself in a series of revolts against Roman rule."[3]

While the leaders were fasting and in prayer, the Holy Spirit instructed them: "Set apart for me Barnabas and Saul for the work to which I have called them" (13:2). This initiated the first of Paul's missionary journeys.

So it was that they made their way to Seleucia, and sailed from there to Cyprus. The island of Cyprus is about 225 kilometers long, and 100 kilometers wide at its broadest point. It is located in the eastern Mediterranean, some 100 kilometers west of the Syrian coastline.

> Cyprus was Barnabas' homeland, it was easily accessible, and almost certainly there were Christians already there (11:19-21; 21:16). John Mark accompanied them (v. 5). His family connection with Barnabas and so, perhaps, with the island, may have been the determining factors in his being chosen.[4]

Luke singles out an incident concerning Elymus the sorcerer for special attention. He was an attendant of the proconsul Sergius Paulus. When Elymus took issue with Paul, the latter accused him: "You are a child of the devil and an enemy of everything that is right! . . . Now the hand of the Lord is against you. You are going to be blind, and for a time you will be unable to see the light of the sun" (13:10-11). When this came to pass, the proconsul believed.

The missionaries subsequently crossed over into Asia Minor, where Paul's first recorded speech was delivered in Pisidian Antioch. It sat astride a main trading route between Ephesus and Cilicia. It had by this time cultivated a pronounced Hellenistic orientation.

The sermon likely suggests the approach Paul would have employed when addressing Jews and God-fearing Gentiles—both familiar with the prophetic tradition. Consequently, he attempts to locate the gospel in terms of salvation history.

"Therefore, my brothers," he earnestly concludes, "I want you to know that through Jesus the forgiveness of sins is proclaimed to you" (13:38). It amounted to an implied invitation.

Almost the whole city was gathered together the next Sabbath to hear *the word of the Lord*. The unbelieving Jews were filled with jealousy, and contradicted what the apostle had to say. "We had to speak the word of God to you first," he countered. "Since you reject it and do not consider yourselves worthy of eternal life, we now turn to the Gentiles." So it was that the word spread throughout the entire region.

At Iconium, Paul and Barnabas (as was their custom) went to the synagogue. Fortuitously located at the edge of a plateau and with an ample water supply, the city prospered. The missionaries spoke so convincingly that many Jews and Gentiles came to faith. Conversely, opposition arose first among the unbelieving Jews and then Gentiles. When it was learned that there was a plan afoot to have them stoned, they fled to the Lyconian cities of Lystra and Derby.

These were relatively obscure and unpretentious. There was at Lystra a man crippled from birth. "Stand to your feet!" Paul commanded him (14:10). At that, the man jumped up and began to walk.

When the crowd witnessed this, they shouted: "The gods have come down to us in human form!" They likely thought that Barnabas was Zeus, because of his more reserved disposition. They readily identified Paul with Hermes, as the spokesman. The populace would have offered sacrifices to them, had they not insisted that it refrain.

Then when unbelieving Jews came from Antioch and Iconium, they incited the crowd against the missionaries. They stoned Paul, and supposing he was dead dragged him outside the city. Once he had recovered, he returned to the city. The next day he and Barnabas left for Derby.

They preached the good news there, with favorable results. After that, they returned to Lystra, Iconium, and Antioch: "strengthening the disciples and encouraging them to remain true to the faith" (14:22). They also appointed elders in each church, commending them to the Lord. Thus concludes Paul's first missionary journey.

Some persons came down from Jerusalem, teaching that it was necessary to be circumcised in order to be saved. The matter was referred to a council convened in Jerusalem. "It is my judgement," James concluded, "that we should not make it difficult for the Gentiles who are turning to God. Instead we should write to them, telling them to abstain from food polluted by idols, from sexual immorality, from the meat of strangled animals and from blood" (15:19-20). Out of deference to the Jews, who would associate such with the course of a righteous Gentile (as derived from God's covenant with Noah). James' reasoning prevailed.

The deliberation of the Jerusalem Council was well received in Antioch. Some time later, Paul suggested to Barnabas: "Let us go back and visit the brothers in all the towns where we preached the word of the Lord and see how they are doing" (15:36). A dispute arose concerning whether to take Mark with them, and so they went their separate ways. With Silas as his companion, Paul now sets out on his second missionary journey.

As elaborated in an earlier context, Paul had a vision concerning a man from Macedonia, pleading for help. They immediately made ready for departure.

Luke first draws our attention to Philippi. It had a military history, and was settled in part by Roman colonists. These continued to enjoy their rights, as if the region were an extension of the Roman peninsula. There Paul and Silas were imprisoned, but miraculously delivered.

They continued on to Thessalonica. Founded by Macedonia to celebrate its victories, it had become the principal city in the region. It was strategically located as a commercial center. Paul made his way to the synagogue, and for three days "reasoned with them from the Scriptures, explaining and proving that the Christ had to suffer and rise from the dead" (17:3). Some of the Jews and God-fearing Gentiles were persuaded.

However, some of the unbelieving Jews created a riot. When they could not find the missionaries, they dragged Jason and some other brothers before the city officials. "These men who have caused trouble all over the world have now come here," they protested. "They are defying Caesar's decrees, saying that there is another king, one called Jesus." The officials made Jason and the others post bond, and let them go their way. It was their intent to prohibit any further disturbance.

Under the cover of night, the believers sent Paul and Silas on to Berea—a distance of about 80 kilometers. It was off the Via Agnatia, and would provide a suitable refuge. It appears to have been a relatively prosperous city at the time, which invited a Jewish presence.

"Now the Bereans were of more noble character than the Thessalonians, for they received the message with great eagerness and examined the Scriptures every day to see if what Paul said was true" (17:11). In a manner of speaking, they exhibited an open mind but not an empty head. Many Jews and Greeks subsequently came to faith.

When the unbelieving Jews in Thessalonica learned that Paul had extended his ministry to Berea, they followed him and began to stir up the populace. As a result, certain of the believers escorted the apostle to Athens, while Silas and Timothy remained behind. In this manner, they hoped to defuse the situation.

Although Athens had long since lost its political prominence, "she continued to represent the highest level of culture attained in classical antiquity. . . . In consideration of her splendid past, the Romans gave Athens the right to maintain her own institutions as a free and allied city within the Roman Empire."[5] Paul reasoned in the synagogue with Jews and God-fearing Gentiles, and in the marketplace with any who happened to be there.

He was given a hearing before the Areopagus. It was an aristocratic body of venerable antiquity, which exercised jurisdiction in matters of religion and morality. "May we know what this new teaching is that you are presenting" they inquired of the apostle. "All the Athenians and the foreigners who lived there spent their time doing nothing but talking about and listening to the latest ideas," Luke observed in this connection.

Pauls' address is perhaps meant to illustrate how he went about reasoning with a pagan audience. "I see that in every way you are very religious," he pointedly observed. "For as I walked around and looked carefully at your objects of worship, I even found an altar with this inscription: **to an unknown god**. Now what you worship as something unknown I am going to proclaim to you."

"The God who made the world and everything in it is the Lord of heaven and earth and does not live in temples built with hands," he continued. "And he is not served by human hands, as if he needed anything, because he himself gives all men life and breath and everything else."

"From one man he made every nation of men, that they should inhabit the whole earth; and he determined the times set for them and the exact places where they should live," he further reasoned. "God did this so that men would seek him and perhaps reach out for him and find him, though he is not far from each one of us. For in him we live and move and have our being."

"In the past God overlooked such ignorance (as cited above), but now he commands all people everywhere to repent." *All people everywhere* falls within the scope of the ingathering of the Gentiles, anticipated by the prophets. Upon hearing this, some ridiculed the apostle, while others asked to hear him again, and a few believed. One would gather from this that it was a hard sell.

Leaving Athens, Paul continued on to Corinth. Corinth was strategically located at the western end of the isthmus between central Greece and the Peloponnesus, so that it became a flourishing center of trade. It was dominated by an acropolis, which in ancient times accommodated the temple of Aphrodite, the goddess of love. All things considered, it cultivated a proverbial immorality.

After an extended stay in Corinth, the apostle set sail for Syria. He subsequently arrived in Ephesus. It was at the time the most important city in the Roman province of Asia. It was also situated at the mouth of the Cayster River, between the mountain range of Coressus and the sea. When asked to extend his time there, he promised: "I will come back if it is God's will." He then set sail for Caesarea, and made his way from there to Antioch. Thus concludes his second missionary journey.

After spending some time in Antioch, the apostle traveled from place to place throughout the region of Galatia and Phrygia, strengthening the disciples. This signaled the beginning of his third missionary journey. He eventually worked his way back to Ephesus. There he encountered disciples of John the Baptist. "Did you receive the Holy Spirit when you believed?" he inquired of them.

"No," they replied, "we have not even heard that there is a Holy Spirit." Whereupon, the apostle instructed them concerning the good news, and they gladly received the indwelling of the Spirit.

He ministered boldly in the synagogue for three months, concerning *the kingdom of God*. When some opposed him, he retired to the lecture hall of Tyrannus. There he continued for two years, "so that all the Jews and Greeks who lived in the province of Asia heard the word of the Lord" (19:10).

He likewise performed many miracles. When this became known, "the name of the Lord was held in high honor. Many of those who believed now came and openly confessed their evil deeds. A number who had practiced sorcery brought their scrolls together and burned them publically."

The apostle subsequently determined to go up to Jerusalem. While he lingered, a silversmith named *Demetrius* incited his fellow craftsmen. "He (Paul) says that man-made gods are no gods at all," he protested.

> There is danger not only that our trade will lose its good name (and the artisans their source of income), but also that the temple of the great goddess Artemis will be discredited, and the goddess herself, who is worshiped throughout the province of Asia and the world, will be robbed of her divine majesty.

Incidently, the temple qualified as one of the seven wonders of the ancient world.

Two of Paul's companions were seized, and rushed into the theater. Paul wanted to join them, but his friends persuaded him not to do so. The assembly was in confusion; most did not even know why they had gathered. They settled for shouting in unison for two hours, "Great is Artemis of the Ephesians!"

"Men of Ephesus," the clerk employed them,

> doesn't all the world know that the city of Ephesus is the guardian of the temple of the great Artemis and her image, which fell from heaven? . . . If, then, Demetrius and his fellow craftsmen have a grievance against anybody, the courts are open and there are proconsuls. . . . As it is, we are in danger of being charged with rioting because of today's events.

After admonishing them, he dismissed the gathering.

When the uproar had ended, Paul set out for Macedonia. His itinerary is sketchy at this point, with the apostle eventually sailing from Philippi to Troas—where he stayed for seven days. He decided to bypass Ephesus, to avoid spending more time in the region. From Melitus, he sent for the Ephesian elders to join him there. Miletus was the most southerly of the Greek cities on the western coast of Asia Minor. It flourished as a commercial center at the time.

"Keep watch over yourselves and all the flock of which the Holy Spirit has made you overseers," he earnestly admonished them. After he had finished speaking, he knelt down with them and prayed. "What grieved them most was his statement they would never see his face again." The curtain thus drops on his third missionary journey.

Paul eventually makes his way up to Jerusalem. This was his fourth arrival recorded by Luke. First, as a young rabbinical student. Second, after his encounter with the risen Lord. Third, as a member of the delegation to the Jerusalem Council. Finally, to initiate what is sometimes characterized as his *passion*, drawing upon its similarity to that of Jesus.

When some of the Jews of the diaspora saw him in the temple precinct they assumed he had profaned the area by bringing Gentiles with him. The Roman security had to rescue him from the incensed populace. When it was learned that there was a conspiracy to put him to death, the commander sent him off with a military escort to Casearea.

Caesarea was constructed by Herod the Great on the site of Strato's Tower, located on the Mediterranean coastline 37 kilometers south of Mount Carmel and about 100 kilometers northwest of Jerusalem. It lay along the international trade route between Tyre and Egypt, providing ample opportunity for maritime and inland commerce. It was also selected as the provincial headquarters for the Roman occupational forces.

After five days, the apostle made a spirited defense before the magistrate Felix. "As Paul discoursed on righteousness, self-control and the judgment to come, Felix was afraid and said, 'That's enough for now! You may leave. When I find it convenient, I will send for you'" (24:25). He was in hopes that Paul would offer him a bribe.

After two years were past, Felix was succeeded by Festus, who wanted to grant the unbelieving Jews a favor by leaving the apostle in prison. He subsequently suggested sending Paul back to Jerusalem to face the charges brought against him. The apostle resolutely responded: "I am standing before Caesar's court, where I ought to be tried. I have not done any wrong to the Jews, as you yourself know very well.... I appeal to Caesar!" (25:10-11).

So it was that Paul boarded a ship, along with other prisoners, bound for Rome. They were shipwrecked along the way, but eventually succeeded in reaching their destination. Rome was at that time going through a prolonged period of rapid growth, and likely had a population of over a million inhabitants.

As previously noted, he was allowed to live in rented quarters over a two-year period. After which, it is supposed that he was released—only to be apprehended again and executed. So the course of Paul's life and teaching appear when viewed *in situ*. Consequently, we can identify with him in some regards, while obviously not in others.

SALVATION HISTORY

"He made known to us the mystery of his will, according to his good pleasure, which he purposed in himself to suitably administer concerning the fullness of the times, under the supervision of Christ, both things in the heavens and things upon the earth in him" (Eph. 1:9-10, free translation). Thus are we alerted to the critical role that *the fullness of times* places in the apostle's thinking. This is coupled with the notion of space as a four-dimensional continuum.

With broad brush strokes, God benevolently provided for man's needs. Man (male and female), however, thought they could improve on the situation. The situation became untenable, and they were banished from God's presence. It remained for God to take the initiative, embracing Abraham and his posterity, as a means of reaching out to all. As Jesus succinctly observed, "salvation is from the Jews" (John 4:22).

In greater detail,

> *telling time* originates in traditional perspective with the Mosaic era, although this would not rule out the use of prior sources. It is far removed from such action time as recorded in the Genesis' account of creation. It is much closer to God's deliverance of his people from bondage in Egypt.[1]

We are thus invited to look back, before tracing events from this critical juncture in salvation history. "In the beginning, God created the heavens and the earth" (Gen. 1:1). *In the beginning* likely corresponds to the time of the gods depicted in extra-biblical sources. As such, before humans came on stage. In this instance, however, when God appears in solitary splendor.

"Now the earth was formless and empty, darkness was over the surface of the deep, and the Spirit of God was hovering over the waters." This appears analogous to the time when a potter casts his clay, before fashioning a vessel. The Spirit hovers expectantly, as the potter's hands pause momentarily before proceeding.

"And God said," and it was accomplished. It was decidedly in a sovereign manner. "And God saw that it was good." Then, in conclusion, "God saw all that he had made, and it was very good" (Gen. 1:31). Such as would imply that it was both functional and aesthetically pleasing.

God planted a garden, placed man within it, and instructed him to tend it. He could eat of its produce, with the exception of the tree of knowledge of good and evil. While variously interpreted, it seems best to consider this a comprehensive idiom (similar to as far as the east is from the west). In this instance, to eat from the tree would be tantamount to declaring one's autonomy.

The result was tragic. This, in turn, recalls John Milton's classic description of the original couple's retreat from their privileged sanctuary:

> They, looking back, all th' eastern side beheld
> Of Paradise, so late their happy seat.
> Waved over by the flaming brand; the gate
> With dreadful faces thronged and fiery arms.
> Some natural tears they dropped, but wiped them soon;
> The world was all before them, where to choose
> Their place of rest, and Providence their guide.
> They, hand in hand, with wandering steps and slow,
> Through Eden took their solitary way.[2]

While alienated, they were not forsaken. *Providence* remained their guide. As aptly observed, it is better to be in the hands of a wrathful God than to fall out of them.

Creation at large was adversely impacted. Paul observes in this regard, "We know that the whole creation has been groaning as in the pains of childbirth right up to the present time" (Rom. 8:22). In anticipation of deliverance and restoration. This is in keeping with chaos theory, since small variations in initial situations have a profound impact on subsequent events.

With the passing of time, "The Lord saw how great man's wickedness on the earth had become, and that every inclination of the thoughts of his heart was only evil all the time" (Gen. 6:5). One could hardly imagine a more sweeping indictment. A great deluge ensued. However, Noah and his family, along with breeding animals were saved through the building of an ark—at God's direction. Whereupon, the Lord announced that he had set the rainbow in the sky as a sign of his covenant with the patriarch. It resembled a bow held overhead as a sign of peace.

"Now the whole world had one language and a common speech" (Gen. 11:1). "Come," they encouraged one another, "let us build ourselves a city, with a tower that reaches to the heavens, so that we may make a name for ourselves and not be scattered over the face of the earth." It was a pretentious endeavor, meant for self-aggrandizement.

God decided to confuse their language, lest they attempt something more counterproductive. "From there the Lord scattered them over the face of the whole earth." This was in anticipation of a time when he would bond them together by way of pouring out the Holy Spirit (cf. Acts 2:1-8).

Now the word of the Lord came to Abram (Abraham):

> Leave your country, your people, and your father's household and go to the land

I will show you. I will make you into a great nation and I will bless you; I will make your name great, and you will be a blessing. I will bless those who bless you, and whoever curses you I will curse; and all peoples on earth will be blessed through you (Gen. 12:1-3).

The succession appears to be increasingly threatening, suggesting the high cost of answering God's summons. Conversely, there would be ample compensation: in terms of a large posterity, lavish blessings, a prized reputation, and shared benefits. "By faith Abraham," it was subsequently remembered, "when called to a place he would later receive as his inheritance, obeyed and went, even though he didn't know where he was going" (Heb. 11:8).

Some time later God sorely tested Abraham. "Take your son, Isaac, whom you love, and go to the region of Moriah. Sacrifice him there as a burnt offering on one of the mountains I will tell you about" (Gen. 22:1-2). We are not told what went through the patriarch's mind, except for the subsequent observation that he believed God could raise the youth from the dead (cf. Heb. 11:9).

When they reached the appointed place, Abraham built an altar, arranged wood on it, bound his son, and laid him on the altar. He was about to sacrifice his beloved son when a voice from heaven called out: "Do not do anything to him. Now I know that you fear God, because you have not withheld from me your son, your only son."

Abraham looked up, and saw a ram caught by its horns in a thicket. He took the ram and sacrificed it in place of his son. This would take proverbial form, "On the mountain of the Lord it will be provided." Moreover, the *akida* (binding of Isaac) would be uniquely recalled by subsequent generations as a precedent for obedience and resolve.

While the patriarchs were appreciatively recalled as men of faith, they were not always faithful. As a result, one could readily identify with them. This came by way of an encouragement to realize that God uses imperfect instruments to achieve his gracious purposes.

While Genesis closes with the Israelites secure in Egypt, Exodus finds them threatened by a new regime. "Look," Pharaoh warned his people, "the Israelites have become much too numerous for us. Come, we must deal shrewdly with them or they will become even more numerous and, if war breaks out, will join our enemies, fight against us and leave the country" (Exod. 1:9-10).

So they pressed the subject people into building store cities. When this failed to compromise their strength, he ordered that any male children be killed at birth. "Jewish expositors have seen parallels to Pharaoh's action in the attempted genocide of Israel by Hitler and others; Christian expositors have sought such parallels in the persecutions suffered by the church throughout her history."[3]

When Moses was born, his mother concealed him. When this no longer seemed feasible, she placed the child in a papyrus basket coated with tar and pitch. She then put it among the reeds along the bank of the Nile, while his sister kept watch. When Pharaoh's daughter went to bathe, she discovered the child, and eventually adopted it.

One day, when Moses was fully grown, he went out to where his people were engaged in hard labor (repeated three times for emphasis). He observed an Egyptian beating a Hebrew, and killed the former. When this became public knowledge, he fled to the region of Midian and escape retaliation.

There he married a daughter of the priest Jethro. He was subsequently tending his father-in-law's flock when he saw a burning bush that was not consumed. The phenomenon has been variously explained, but need not concern us. When Moses drew near the bush, a voice commanded him: "Take off your sandals, for the place where you are standing is holy ground" (Exod. 3:5).

After that, the voice explained: "I am the God of your father, the God of Abraham, the God of Isaac and the God of Jacob." The Lord then confided, "I have indeed seen the misery of my people in Egypt.... So I have come down to rescue them from the hand of the Egyptians and to bring them out of that land into a good and spacious land, a land flowing with milk and honey (pastoral imagery indicative of abundance)."

"Egypt was one of the most powerful nations on earth and was proud of its heritage and religions. But by means of the ten plagues, Pharaoh and his people learned the hard way there was no one like the God of Israel, who was supreme in heaven and earth (cf. 7:5; 9:14)."[4] The chosen people were also assured of the Lord's gracious sovereignty, and told to recall his faithfulness from one generation to the next.

The third month after the Israelites left Egypt, they arrived at the Desert of Sinai. They encamped there at the foot of a prominent elevation. Moses went up to meet with God, while the people remained below. God subsequently instructed him to say to the populace: "You yourselves have seen what I did to Egypt, and how I carried you on eagles' wings, and brought you to myself. Now if you obey me fully and keep my covenant, then out of all nations you will be my treasured possession (Exod. 19:4-5). Such as would qualify as *a kingdom of priests*, and *a holy nation*.

The significance of the decalogue can hardly be overstated. The rabbis

> speculated that it was prepared on the eve of creation in anticipation of subsequent use; they asserted that as each commandment was sounded from the lofty height of Sinai it filled the world with a pleasing aroma; they concluded that all nature hushed to hear every word as it was spoken.[5]

While the commandments were *apodictic* (pertaining to general principles) in character, the extended covenant embraced *casuistic* regulations as well (regarding specific applications). In all, it resembled a vassal treaty, and thus consisted of an introduction, historical prelude, stipulations (constituting the bulk of the covenant), blessings and cursings, and provision for renewal.

On the twentieth day of the second month of the second year, the people left Sinai—bound for the promised land (cf. Num. 10:11). God subsequently instructed Moses to send out spies to report on their findings. "We went into the land to which you sent us, and it does flow with milk and honey!" they exclaimed. "But the people who live there are powerful, and the cities are fortified and very large."

The folk were intimidated. They would not be pacified, and refused to settle in the land. As a result, a generation was condemned to wander aimlessly in the wilderness.

They again approached the promised land. "Be strong and courageous," the Lord encouraged Joshua, "because you will lead these people to inherit the land I swore to their forefathers to give them" (Joshua 1:6).

Nevertheless, they failed to purge the land of its previous inhabitants—as they had been instructed. Whereupon, there intervened the turbulent time of the judges. "In those days Israel had no king; everyone did as he saw fit" (Judges 21:25). In other words, anarchy prevailed.

A common cycle reoccurs throughout the narratives. Initially, the Israelites do evil in the sight of the Lord. Then, since they could not restrain sin within, they could not contain evil without. Consequently, they were oppressed by others. As a result, they cried out to the Lord. He would respond by sending them a deliverer, after which they enjoyed peace for a time—before succumbing again to their evil ways.

The time came when the people desired a king to rule over them, after the fashion of those who lived around them. While this reflected a lack of trust in the Almighty, their request was granted. Hence, it would be necessary to fine-tune the monarchy to the conditions of the covenant. This burden would especially fall upon the school of the prophets.

The early rulers started well, but subsequently floundered. The kingdom was torn in two. The northern kingdom went into decline from the outset. It was just a matter of time before invading Assyrians overwhelmed all resistance, and resettled the people. The southern kingdom fared better. It enjoyed times of spiritual renewal, before eventually succumbing to the Babylonians. The privileged class was whisked away into captivity, while a residue of common folk were left to cope with a situation said to resemble primal chaos (cf. Gen. 1:2; Jer. 4:23).

The prophets, who had warned of the impending disaster, now turned to consoling the people. Along this line, encouraging them to make the best of a difficult situation, and in anticipation of a return from exile. The latter would eventually come to pass, in terms of what is said to resemble a new exodus.

Even so, the school of the prophets soon withered on the vine. It was as if God had decided that it would no longer serve any constructive purpose to appeal to his wayward people. This ushered in an interim variously described as *the silent years*, and a time of travail—as a prelude to the advent of the Messiah and pervasive *shalom* (peace, well-being).

Meanwhile, there were other fortuitous events taking place. Hellenism had spread throughout the ancient Near East, providing a ready means for communicating among diverse peoples. So much so, that it was said that to simply breathe was to encounter Hellenic culture.

This development was variously received by the Jewish people. While some saw it as a way of embracing a more cosmopolitan and enlightened attitude, others thought it a serious threat to cherished traditions. The controversy was raging as a prelude to the birth of Jesus.

The Roman Empire also paved the way for the rise of the Christian movement. Initially, in terms of the *Pax Romana* (peace of Rome). This provided a degree of civility largely lacking elsewhere. All else was thought to be barbaric.

Then, too, the Romans maintained an intricate system of roadways. This not only facilitated travel, but provided a relatively safe means. All things considered, it was a testimony to the practical Roman mentality.

Now it came to pass that there were shepherds tending their flocks by night when "An angel of the Lord appeared to them, and the glory of the Lord shone around them, and they were terrified" (Luke 2:9). "Do not be afraid," the angel encouraged them. "Today in the town of David a Savior has been born to you; he is Christ the Lord." When the shepherds had seen for themselves, "they spread the word concerning what had been told them about the child, and all who heard it were amazed at what the shepherds said to them."

This is an appropriate time to take inventory. There was the infant Jesus. The event was shrouded with Messianic ambiguity. Most appealing was the notion that the Messiah would perpetuate the dynasty of David. In this role, he would establish order and thwart the ambition of hostile neighbors. Until such time as he would subject all to the righteous rule of the Almighty.

There was also the alternative image of a suffering servant. This was less appealing than the previous portrait, and sometimes attributed to Israel as a whole. Not necessarily to the exclusion of an individual, who might be representative of the rest. When coupled together, it gave rise to the idea of there being two Messiahs, one of royal and the other of priestly character.

There was Bethlehem. It was a likely place for one of the lineage of David to be born. However, there appeared to be nothing special about the child per se. He wore no halo, nor did he glow with some mysterious radiance (not at this early point in his life). While every birth was perceived as a gift from God, the special character of this gift was yet to be realized.

There were the shepherds. They were likely non-observant Jews (as described in the gospel narratives, *sinners*). As such, they seem to anticipate that the good news was meant for all people, and not simply the religious elite. This, moreover, was borne out in the angelic pronouncement of peace on all whom God's favor rests (cf. Luke 2:24).

There were the religiously meticulous, conspicuous by their absence. They carried on their appointed ritual, oblivious to the fact that something out of the ordinary had transpired. One gets the impression that they took pleasure in a religious pecking order, which pampered their self-righteousness.

Since we have considered the Jesus of history at some length, we need only tie salvation together with a brief resume. There were the obscure years, wherein Jesus grew from a child to a man. There was little out of the ordinary, except that Jesus appears exemplary and attentive to his calling.

He was about thirty years of age when he began his public ministry. Persons initially remarked about how he taught with authority, rather than rely on religious precedent—as was the rabbinic custom. They were likely hard pressed to come up with a satisfactory explanation.

He soon performed remarkable feats. This was not at issue, although some attributed them to the working of Satan. "If Satan drives out Satan, he is divided against himself," Jesus observed. "But if I drive out demons by the Spirit of God, then the kingdom of God has come upon you" (Matt. 12:26, 28).

In addition, he assumed the prerogative to forgive sin. Whereupon, certain of the scribes concluded that he was blaspheming. "Which is easier to say, 'Your sins are forgiven' or to say, 'Get up and walk'? Jesus inquired. "But so that you may know that the Son of Man has authority on earth to forgive sins . . . ," his voice appears to have trailed off (Matt. 9:5-6).

The initial response to Jesus seems to have been overtly favorable. He spoke engagingly. His message expressed good news, in notable contrast to that of John the Baptist—who warned of impending judgment. He was sensitive to the needs of those around him. He was patient with honest seekers.

However, with the passing of time, opposition built. Jesus now appeared as a serious threat to the status quo. Had he been an advocate of cheap grace, no doubt the results would have been different. Sin offers a form of security.

In proverbial terms, the handwriting was on the wall. Jesus warned his disciples about what would befall him in Jerusalem, after which he would be raised from the dead. Peter attempted to dissuade him, but to no avail. Thomas suggested that they perish with him, but it was not to be.

They crucified him, as if a common thief. Conversely, there was nothing with which to charge him, except for his being the king of the Jews. When the Jewish leaders urged Pilate to alter the inscription to say that he claimed to be king of the Jews, the Roman magistrate would not relent. Jesus died, as he had lived, submissive to the will of his heavenly Father.

This was not the end. Three days later he was reported to be alive. He appeared from time to time, encouraging his disciples. He likewise instructed them to remain in Jerusalem until endued with power from on high, after which they were to disciple all nations. Even then, it took severe persecution to scatter them throughout Judea and Samaria. They went proclaiming the good news.

Paul eventually assumed center stage. He was a person peculiarly prepared by a combination of factors to serve as the apostle to the Gentiles. One thing was missing: a personal encounter with the risen Lord. This transpired as he was on his way to Damascus to extend his persecution of the followers of Jesus.

It would not be the end, but the beginning of the end. Jesus promised to return in glory, and thus to triumph over the resistive forces of evil. This serves as a caution to those who are complacent in their evil ways, and as an encouragement to those who pursue righteousness. So it is that the expression *in Christ* appears in the context of salvation history, and more expressly, regarding the fullness of times.

THE ANGELS' VIEW

"Blessed be the God and Father of our Lord Jesus Christ, who has blessed us with every spiritual blessing from above in Christ," Paul enthusiastically writes (Eph. 1:3, free translation). This, in turn, recalls J. B. Phillips' provocative account of the discussion between two angels concerning what had transpired. That is to say, as things appeared from the privileged vantage point of heaven's ramparts.

Now when Jesus had finished speaking to his disciples, "he was taken up before their very eyes, and a cloud hid him from their sight" (Acts 1:9). "When he ascended on high," Paul elaborates, "he led captives in his train and gave gifts to me" (Eph. 4:8; cf. Psa. 68:18). As if a victor, returning to the acclaim of the populace, along with tokens of his conquest.

Three resilient themes can be readily detected in the extended passage. "First, from eternity to eternity God works all things according to his perfect plan. All history, all people, all that exists in heaven and on earth are included in his purpose."[1] The good and the bad, the momentous and the inconsequential, the prolonged and the momentary; indeed, all things!

We are not necessarily aware of how God is providentially working in our lives (cf. Rom. 8:28). Sometimes it seems little more than a matter of fortuitous timing. On other occasions, only upon subsequent reflection. In any case, in an eminently creative fashion.

Second, God's ultimate purpose is achieved in Christ.

> The scientific prediction of cosmic futility simply reminds us that a king of evolutionary optimism—a belief that the unfolding of history must bring progress to fulfilment—is inadequate as a ground of hope. If there really is a sure and lasting hope, it can only rest in the eternal being of God himself.[2]

If fulfilled in Christ, then eminently well done. While proof texts abound, Paul was consoled with the assurance: "My grace is sufficient for you, for my power is made perfect in weakness" (2 Cor. 12:9). "Therefore I will boast all the more gladly about my weaknesses, so that Christ's power may rest on me," the apostle aptly concludes.

Finally, the goal has practical implications. "Since, then, you have been raised with Christ, set your hearts on things above, where Christ is seated at the right hand of God," Paul admonishes (Col. 3:1). *Since then* points to an indeterminate time in the past, one that differs from one person to the next.

Christ is the common denominator in Christian conversion. In him old things have passed away, and all has become new. As a result, one is no longer bound by licentious desires and temporal pursuits. He or she is rather enamored of spiritual realities, and engaged in a rigorous spiritual pilgrimage.

One is enjoined to set his or her mind on things above. In greater detail, "clothe yourselves with compassion, kindness, humility, gentleness and patience. Bear with each other and forgive whatever grievances you have against one another.... And over all these virtues put on love, which binds them all together in perfect unity" (vv. 12, 14). Love thus appears as an indispensable catalyst.

"Let the peace of Christ rule in your hearts, since as members of one body you were called to peace" (v. 15). Recall in this regard Jesus' word of encouragement to his disciples: "Peace I leave with you; my peace I give you. I do not give to you as the world gives. Do not let your hearts be troubled and do not be afraid" (John 14:27).

"Let the word of Christ dwell in you richly as you teach and admonish one another with all wisdom, and as you sing psalms" (v. 16). The *word of Christ* appears objective, thus recalling his detailed instruction. In more extended fashion, this serves for instruction, exhortation, and celebration.

"And whatever you do, whether in word or deed, do it all in the name of the Lord Jesus, giving thanks to God the Father through him" (v. 17). *Whatever* allows for no exceptions. *In the name* implies being in accord with all that Jesus had undertaken, and commended to faithful followers. Then in a thankful spirit, rather than begrudgingly; while drawing upon one's privileged relationship with and through Christ.

A text from Hebrews next invites our attention. It seems probable that Hebrews was written by someone associated with Paul in his apostolic mission, and if so, highly compatible with his way of reasoning. "Therefore, since we have a great high priest who has gone through the heavens, Jesus the Son of God, let us hold firmly to the faith we profess," the author admonishes.

> For we do not have a high priest who is unable to sympathize with our weaknesses, but we have one who has been tempted in every way, just as we are—yet without sin. Let us then approach the throne of grace with confidence, so that we may receive mercy and find grace to help us in our time of need (Heb. 4:14-16).

A great high priest singles Jesus out from the rest, given the before-mentioned angelic perspective. Since he has been grandly exalted, having passed through the heavens. There he continues to intercede on behalf of the faithful, in contrast to those who must offer periodic sacrifices.

Additionally,

The Son is not at first identified with Jesus, but there is an initial build-up which impressively presents the Son's exalted status. He is heir of all things, creator, reflector of God's glory; he bears the stamp of God's nature, upholds the universe in his power, has purged sins and has been enthroned at God's right hand.[3]

All of this is in keeping with the traditional notion that a son reveals the character of his father. According to conventional wisdom, "Like father, like son."

Since we have such a high priest, let us hold fast to the faith we profess. Act on the basis of our convictions. Do not grow weary in the pursuit of righteousness. Maintain a good pace, and finish strong.

Let us also bear in mind that Jesus can readily identify with our human frailties. Since he humbled himself by taking human form and becoming submissive to death. In that he has been there, he can be there for us.

This, in turn, recalls talking with a person who from time to time was institutionalized for emotional problems. "Of course," he observed, "I would prefer that this were not necessary. However, I find that at such times I can minister to patients with similar disorders, growing out of our common malady." Something of this sort seems implied concerning Jesus' availability.

Since we have such a high priest, let us also confidently approach the throne of grace. Do not hold back, as if uncertain what sort of reception we will receive. Approach the *throne of grace*, as the source of unmerited favor. If for no other reason than we are admonished to do so.

As for additional commentary,

> the presence of the Christians' high priest on the heavenly throne of grace bespeaks a work of atonement completed not in token but in fact, and the constant availability of divine aid in all their need. Thanks to him, the throne of God is a mercy-seat to which they have free access and from which they may receive all the grace and power required 'for timely help' in the hour of trial and crisis.[4]

"I really don't know *what* is happening," Helmut Thielicke freely admits. "But I do know about the theme in the *name* of which it happens. I know the heart of Him who holds the drama of history and my life together within that theme, steadily carrying it through to its last act."[5] All else seems of relatively little consequence.

Still, it helps to put matters in divine perspective. "I tell you the truth," Jesus solemnly declared, "anyone who has faith in me will do what I have been doing. He will do even greater things than these, because I am going to the Father" (John 14:12). Not as a result of our autonomous endeavor, but through his effective intercession.

"All this I have spoken while still with you," Jesus allows. "But the Counselor, the Holy Spirit, whom the Father will send in my name, will teach you all things, and remind you of everything I have said to you" (vv. 25-26). The Holy Spirit thus assumes the role of mentor, in keeping with the truth that has already been revealed.

Moreover, as the agent for sanctification. Assuming in this regard that persons are works in progress. Then, not in retreat from the world, but through engagement.

In a manner some have described as *worldly sanctity*.

"It is not for you to know the times or dates the Father has set by his own authority," Jesus subsequently informed them. "But you will receive power when the Holy Spirit comes on you; and you will be my witnesses in Jerusalem, and in all Judea and Samaria, and to the ends of the earth" (Acts 1:7-8). *You will receive power* implies a transformation of significant magnitude.

This might be understood in either a subjective or objective sense, but likely meant to embrace both. As for the former, they would be infused with a holy boldness. As a result, they would fearlessly proclaim the word of life. Faced with incredible obstacles, they would persist in the mission entrusted to them.

As for the latter, they would reap a bountiful harvest. In this connection, there were by 250 A.D. about one million adherents—constituting about two percent of the populace of the Roman Empire. Fifty years later the number had risen to six million, approximately ten percent of the population.

They were to tarry in Jerusalem. The scene of Jesus' demise and triumphant resurrection. In Judea and Samaria thereafter, incited by persecution. Finally, to the ends of the earth. Thus to expand their efforts to the far horizons, and all that intervened.

The task was exceedingly formidable. If for no other reason than simple logistics. The disciples at first constituted only a small cluster of the faithful. They were drawn from a people not uncommonly depreciated. They were for the most part Galileans, thought less sophisticated than their Judean counterparts.

The problem was compounded by misunderstanding. The disciples were thought irreligious, since they refused to participate in pagan worship. They were charged with cannibalistic rites, derived from their communion liturgy. They were thought to hate the human race, because they warned of impending judgment.

The task was made still more difficult via contrived hostility. "From the beginning of persecution to the time of Decius in 250, all persecution was local. In 202, Septimius Severus forbade conversion to Christianity; Maximinus Thrax (225-238) ordered clergy to be executed. However, their decrees were only partially carried out."[6] From the time of Nero to that of Constantine, there was persecution from time to time, and with various degrees of severity.

"When the day of Pentecost was fully come, they were all gathered together in one place" (Acts 21:1). The designation is derived from it occurring on the fiftieth day after Passover. It was originally a harvest celebration, and would eventually become associated with the giving of the Torah. The combined symbolism seems apt for the pouring out of the Spirit.

"Suddenly a sound like the blowing of a violent wind came from heaven and filled the whole house where they were sitting. They saw what seemed to be tongues of fire that separated and came to rest on each of them." The description is analogical. All things considered, the account is reminiscent of the Old Testament theophany (cf. Exod. 19:16-19).

"All of them were filled with the Holy Spirit and began to speak in other tongues as the Spirit enabled them." This, in turn, recalls the prophecy that God would pour out his spirit on *all people* (Acts 2:17; Joel 2:28). It is not clear from the syntax whether all spoke with tongues, or only some of them. The latter seems more likely.

Other tongues lacks a more precise definition, except that certain persons heard them speaking in their native languages. This, however, could be variously explained. As a result, we are left to speculate whether it was ecstatic utterance, actual language, or some combination of the two.

Ecstatic utterance is, as the designation implies, articulation associated with ecstatic experience and/or conditioned behavior. While not a language as such, it follows a cultural pattern. It is a common phenomenon, not limited to Christian expression. As an example, that which was reported concerning the Delphi Oracle.

It should also be noted that persons on occasion include elements of a foreign language during ecstasy. This is said to result from suppressed memory, and is characteristically unintelligible to the speaker. Consequently, it would require interpretation. In any case, there is no indication that the Holy Spirit endued persons with the ability to speak a foreign language as a matter of course.

What seems eminently certain is that the incident was meant to symbolize the restoration of language, diffused at the Tower of Babel. In times past, God had confounded their language so that they would be scattered, and their presumption thwarted. Now he draws diverse people together into a common fellowship.

"What does this mean?" some inquired. Others, however, supposed that they were intoxicated. Given their ecstatic state and accompanying behavior. Whereupon, Peter stood up with the Eleven, and raised his voice for all to hear: "Fellow Jews and all of you who live in Jerusalem, let me explain this to you . . . . These men are not drunk, as you suppose. . . . No, this is what was spoken by the prophet Joel"—concerning the last days when God would pour out his spirit.

"Men of Israel," he subsequently continued: "Jesus of Nazareth was a man accredited by God to you by miracles, wonders and signs, which God did among you through him, as you yourselves know." It was common knowledge, although variously attributed—whether to God or Satan.

"This man was handed over to you by God's set purpose and foreknowledge, and you, with the help of wicked men, put him to death by nailing him to the cross. But God raised him from the dead, freeing him from the agony of death, because it was impossible for death to keep its hold on him." While the perpetrators were serving God's redemptive purposes, they were no less accountable for their despicable actions.

In proverbial manner, "While man proposes, God disposes." So it would seem, since God raised Jesus from the dead. Death personified was unable to restrain him. Whereupon, the apostle alludes to the Psalter: "Therefore my heart is glad and my tongue rejoices; my body also will live in hope, because you will not abandon me to the grave, nor will you let your Holy One see decay" (vv. 26-27; cf. Psa. 16:9-10).

The psalm is attributed to David. Consequently, Peter reasons that he must not have been speaking concerning himself, since he is dead and buried—as his tomb bears witness. Whether this makes reference to the site currently bearing that designation on the Western Hill in Jerusalem is a matter of conjecture.

"God has raised this Jesus to life, and we are all witnesses of this fact. Exalted to the right hand of God, he has received from the Father the promised Holy Spirit and has poured out what you now see and hear." Thus the pouring out of the Spirit provides compelling evidence of the fact that Jesus has assumed a place of power and authority, from which he may expand his influence.

When the people heard this, they were *cut to the heart*. "Brothers," they earnestly inquired, "what shall we do?"

"Repent and be baptized, every one of you, in the name of Jesus Christ for the forgiveness of sins," Peter pointedly replied. "And you will receive the gift of the Holy Spirit. The promise is for you and your children and for all who are far off—for all whom the Lord your God will call." *Baptism* is expressly associated with *repentance*, coupled with *faith*—as implied by their inquiry.

You and your children implies a corporate response; hence, not restricted to those present on that occasion. Those *who are far off* appears in context as a reference to Jews of the diaspora, but Peter may well have had in mind the Gentiles as well. The allusion to the Lord's calling serves as a reminder of what is described as *prevenient* (enabling) *grace*. It is not the apostle's intent to imply that persons can make a spiritual recovery apart from God's gracious involvement.

"Save yourself from this corrupt generation," the apostle continues to exhort them. In so doing, to validate the role of human decision in the process. Man's participation is not only solicited but required. "Those who accepted his message were baptized, and about three thousand were added to their number that day." This was a substantial response, given the modest size of the Jewish sectarian movement at that time.

No doubt the angels enjoy a privileged perspective on the redemptive drama being enacted. "Now we see but a poor reflection as in a mirror; then we shall see face to face," Paul observes. "Now I know in part; then I shall know even as I am fully known" (1 Cor. 13:12).

It comes down to this: Christians enjoy *high ground*, from which to carry on the spiritual conflict being waged in the present. Christ is exalted, and the Holy Spirit indwells. Consequently, "Put on the whole armor of God, so that you can take your stand against the devil's schemes" (Eph. 6:11). As expressed in the memorable lyrics of Martin Luther:

> Did we in our own strength confide, our striving would be losing,
> were not the right man on our side, the man of God's own choosing.
> Dost ask who that may be? Christ Jesus, it is he; Lord Sabaoth his name,
> from age to age the same, and he must win the battle (*A Mighty Fortress Is Our God*).

PAUL AS PARADIGM

"Therefore I urge you to imitate me," Paul exhorts his readers (1 Cor. 4:16). "This clause takes the father-child imagery a step further, and in so doing enunciates the point of the entire paragraph . . . . The picture is one of a father who has instructed his children in proper behavior by his own example."[1]

"Follow my example," Paul subsequently adds by way of emphasis, "as I follow the example of Christ" (1 Cor. 11:1). Jesus remains the norm, while the apostle is only an imperfect replica. Dietrich Bonhoeffer likely had something of this in mind when he repudiated the idea of cultivating his own disciples.

"Join with others in following my example, brothers," the apostle exhorts on still another occasion, "and take note of those who love according to the pattern we gave you. For, as I have often told you before and say again even with tears, many live as enemies of the cross of Christ" (Phil. 3:17-18). Here the imagery seems to take on that of rabbinic instruction. The student is meant to emulate his mentor not only in theory but practice. Thereby to honor one's instructor.

Not all are so disposed. They resist the claims of Christ, and in so doing they become *enemies of the cross*. These mind earthly things, while ignoring spiritual realities. "Their destiny is destruction, their god is their stomach, and their glory is their shame." Paul thus assigns them a failing grade.

What the apostle makes explicit on these occasions, is implicit in much of his teaching. He would have persons emulate his manner of life, as an expression of being in Christ. In short, he assumes the role of paradigm.

In greater detail, how was this perceived by those who took his admonition seriously? For an answer to this question, we turn to the early church fathers. In select instances, as necessitated by the breadth of the topic, and with relatively brief commentary.

Initially, we turn our attention to Tertullian. He was born around the year 160 at Carthage, into a pagan Roman family. He was educated in rhetoric and law. He became a Christian prior to the year 197, and wrote extensively in defense of the Christian faith.

Likewise, he became involved with the Montanist controversy. This constituted a revival of prophecy, and a strict adherence to discipline. While there is no convincing evidence that he actually joined the movement—as sometimes asserted, he stoutly defended it against adamant critics.

"You will find no church of apostolic origin but such as reposes its Christian faith in the Creator," Tertullian assures his readers.[2] Note the deference he gives to the apostles, in that he assumes that their teaching is normative for Christians of subsequent generations. This was in context of insisting that it was not Paul's intent to introduce some new God. He is thereby joined with the other apostles in a common enterprise; hence, to faithfully adhere to the God revealed by the patriarchs and prophets.

"What does the Scripture say?" the apostle inquires by way of illustration. "Abraham believed God, and it was credited to him as righteousness" (Rom. 4:3; cf. Gen. 15:6). A righteousness appropriated by faith and manifest by obedience, and not one to the exclusion of the other.

So that he is the father of both Jews and Gentiles, all who walk by faith. "As it is written, 'I have made you a father of many nations'" (v. 17; cf. Gen. 17:5). The promise assumes an essential continuity throughout the course of salvation history, from Genesis to Revelation.

Tertullian elsewhere cites Paul's salutation, as the latter declares himself to be "an apostle not of men, neither by man, but through Jesus Christ and God the Father" (Gal. 1:1).[3] As an apostle of *Jesus Christ and God the Father*, therefore beholden to them. Conversely, not enlisted by men, and so not ultimately obligated to further their diverse agendas.

He thus bears witness to Jesus as the Christ. There had been and would be many pretenders. The church fathers were well aware of this dilemma, since it continued to plague their enterprise.

He also embraces God as Father. As such, the legitimate authority figure. One whose will should take precedent over other concerns. Furthermore, one who sees to it that infractions are not ignored, and compliance rewarded. As might be expected from an ardent advocate of justice.

Moreover, one who is genuinely concerned for his offspring. In that he is not content to let us settle for something inferior. Although he is remarkably patient, being ready to forgive and restore.

Conversely, the child is obligated to obey. Not simply when he or she can grasp what is implicated, but when uncertain. Not only with regard to seemingly critical issues, but those that appear less significant. According to rabbinic thinking, if we obey in lesser matters, the practice is calculated to carry over into more profound concerns. The reverse is also true.

Paul was such a person. "So, then, I was not disobedient to the vision from heaven," he pointedly acknowledges. "First to those in Damascus, then to those in Jerusalem and in all Judea, and to the Gentiles also, I preached that they should repent and turn to God and prove their repentance by their deeds" (Acts 26:19-20). Consequently, it was in keeping with his calling.

"Now, brothers, I want to remind you of the gospel I preached to you, which you received and on which you have taken your stand," the apostle writes along a related line. "For what I received I passed on to you as of first importance: that Christ died for our sins, according to the Scriptures, that he was buried, that he was raised on the third day according to the Scriptures, and that he appeared to various persons and on sundry occasions (1 Cor. 15:1, 3-4).

It therefore comes as no surprise that the church fathers recognized Paul as a faithful herald of the gospel. An early work attributed to Athenagoras (identified as an Athenian, philosopher, and Christian) serves to illustrate. In this regard, he sets out to distinguish the resurrection from immortality of the soul. He reasons as follows:

> His power is sufficient for the raising of dead bodies is shown by the creation of these same bodies. For if, when they did not exist, He made at their first formation the bodies of men. . . . He will, when they are dissolved, in whatever manner that may take place, raise them again and with equal ease: for this, too, is equally possible to Him.[4]

So it would appear from the perspective of one who seeks to emulate the apostle in proclaiming the resurrection. Christ appears as the first-fruit, and the remainder in due time. As Jesus reminded his devious antagonists, "He is not the God of the dead but of the living" (Matt. 22:32).

Irenaeus was Greek, born in Asia Minor into a Christian family. He eventually succeeded the venerable Polycarp as the bishop of Smyrna. He is thought to have died around the beginning of the third century. His main contribution lay in the refutation of heresy, and the exposition of apostolic Christianity.

In the course of his ministry, he encountered the Ebionites, who advocated strict observance of the law. As a result, they were reluctant to admit Paul to the apostolic circle. Irenaeus takes issue with their disclaimer:

> For neither can they contend that Paul was no apostle, when he was chosen for this purpose; nor can they prove Luke guilty of falsehood, when he proclaims the truth to us with all diligence. . . . His testimony, therefore, is true, and the doctrine of the apostles is open and steadfast, holding nothing in reserve; nor did they teach one set of doctrines in private and another in public.[5]

At issue was especially the apostle's stance on Christian liberty. For instance, "It is for freedom that Christ has set us free. Stand firm, then, and do not let yourselves be burdened again by a yoke of slavery" (Gal. 5:1).

> The free grace of God which Paul proclaimed is free grace in more senses than one—free in the sense that it is sovereign and unfettered, free in the sense that it is held forth to men and women for their acceptance by faith alone, and free in the sense that it is the source and principle of their liberation from all kinds of inward and spiritual bondage, including the bondage of legalism and the bondage of moral anarchy.[6]

Free in the sense of being *sovereign and unfettered*. As God meant it to be from the beginning, and before encumbered by sin. Hence, liberated from bondage to sin. On the other hand, free to live toward God and others; in the cause of all that is right and without fear of demise.

Free also in the sense of being enabled to embrace God's gift of salvation. Regardless of merit, without negotiation or excuse, at a given moment in time, and circumstances notwithstanding. This was in accordance with Paul's teaching, and personal example.

Free, finally, to walk in Christian liberty. Whereupon, motivated by love, and exercising creative righteousness. In the stirring words of Martin Luther King: "Free at last! Free at Last! Thank God, I am free at last!" So it would appear from the perspective of Paul as paradigm.

Irenaeus additionally portrays Paul as an emissary of truth. "Finally, brothers, whatever is true, whatever is noble, whatever is right, whatever is pure, whatever is lovely, whatever is admirable—if anything is excellent or praiseworthy—think about such things" (Phil. 4:8). *Whatever is true* serves as the vanguard, as an exhortation to reflect on truth.

Such was meant to cultivate speaking the truth. As for elaboration, "the whole truth, and nothing but the truth." John Calvin was of the opinion that any effort to deceive constitutes a lie.

Finally, to live according to the truth. As if to confirm that what we say is indeed true. This serves to caution the wicked, and encourage the righteous. It is in any case well-pleasing to the Almighty.

Irenaeus also cites Paul by way of protesting those who boast concerning their religious experience. Along this line:

> But since he (Paul) has described that assumption of himself up to the third heaven as something great and pre-eminent, it cannot be that these men ascend above the seventh heaven, for they are certainly not superior to the apostle. If they do maintain that they are more excellent than he, let them prove themselves by their works.[7]

It cannot be that they have ascended *above the seventh heaven*, since there is no such thing. If, however, contrary to fact, they insist; then let them demonstrate their experience by matching the apostle's zealous endeavor. This, too, seems highly unlikely.

It comes as no surprise that the church fathers picked up on the connection between the exaltation of Christ, and the outpouring of the Spirit. We turn to Origin in this regard. He was born around 185 to Christian parents living in Alexandria. His father was martyred. Origin wrote to encourage his father to remain true to the faith, and had to be restrained from joining him.

He was subsequently appointed the director of the catechetical school in Alexandria, and later moved to Caesarea. He was imprisoned during the Decian persecution (249-251), and tortured in an attempt to force him to renounce his faith. He refused to recant, and died a few years after being released from injuries received. He made good use of such time as was given him to write extensively.

"From which it most clearly follows that there is no difference in the Trinity," he deliberately points out, "but that which is called the gift of the Spirit (according to Paul) is made through the Son, and operated by God the Father."[8] Expressly as concerns the variety of gifts made available to the Christian fellowship, and meant to be appreciatively cultivated.

"Now the body is not made up of one part but of many," the apostle reasoned along this line (1 Cor. 12:14). So that the eye cannot say concerning the hand, "I have no need of you." Each is necessary to the working of the whole. "Are all apostles? Paul rhetorically inquires. Obviously not. "Are all teachers, workers of miracles, and the like?" Assuredly not. It is the one Spirit working through all.

It was also observed that Paul gave instruction concerning worship. For instance, "Let us note also that the Apostle had 'delivered' unto the Corinthians (1 Cor. 11:23), as doubtless to others (7:17), certain institutions which he *ordained* in all the churches, and for departing from which he censures the Corinthians . . . in certain particulars."[9] This gave rise to what was described as *The Pauline Norm*. In particular:

1. Supplications.
2. Prayers, Psalms, Hymns, and Spiritual Songs.
3. Intercessions.
4. General Thanksgiving. The Kiss of Peace.
5. Anaphora (concerning the institution of the Lord's Supper).
6. The Lord's Prayer.
7. Communion.

For all the deference shown to the apostle, the church fathers were not unmindful of his human limitations. For instance, Irenaeus observes: "From many other instances also, we may discover that the apostle frequently used a transposed order in his sentences, due to the rapidity of his discourses, and the impetus of the Spirit which was in him."[10] As if a person whose unbridled enthusiasm could hardly be contained.

Such could readily be gathered from the references to Paul's life and ministry. How he labored relentlessly in the work of the Lord. How he experienced privation and persecution. Then, too, how he managed by the grace of the Lord to triumph over seemingly overwhelming obstacles.

The church fathers do not always refer to Paul by name. For instance, Tertullian speculates: "Then, if we are to be caught up alone with them, surely we shall likewise be changed together with them (cf. 1 Thess. 4:17)."[11] Thereby to identify himself with the Pauline tradition.

Then, in turn, to recognize that the apostle was a person oriented toward the future. He was focused on the blessed hope of the Lord's return; hence, not content to sit idly by, but actively engaged in the harvest. Thus comforted but assuredly not complacent.

Paul in the role of martyr was also an exceedingly prominent theme. As an example, Tertullian appreciatively recalls:

But now Paul, an apostle, from being a persecutor, who first of all shed the blood of the church, though afterwards he exchanged the sword for the pen, and turned the dagger into a plough, being *first* a ravening wolf of Benjamin, then himself supply food as did Jacob, how he speaks in favor of martyrdoms, now to be chosen by himself also.[12]

"For I am already being poured out like a drink offering, and the time has come for my departure," the apostle asserts. "I have fought the good fight, I have finished the race, I have kept the faith. Now there is in store for me the crown of righteousness, which the Lord, the righteous Judge, will award to me on that day—and not only to me, but also to all who have longed for his appearing" (2 Tim. 4:6-8).

Rather than pursuing the paper trail further, we will turn to the innovative account of Paul and Thecla as a means to drawing loose ends together. Tertullian asserts that the account was composed by a presbyter, who meant to eulogize the apostle. While likely a fictional character, Thecla was highly esteemed as a model of Christian virtue.

We are alerted to the fact that Onesiphorus expectantly awaited the apostle's arrival. An enthusiastic celebration ensued. Paul seized the opportunity to encourage and exhort those present. A certain virgin named *Thecla* was among them, and listened intently. Her mother was distressed that she might opt for celibacy, and reported the matter to her betrothed.

He, in turn, had the apostle brought before the tribunal. "O proconsul," he appealed, "this man, who he is we know not, who makes virgins averse to marriage; let him say before you on what account he teaches these things."[13]

When given permission to speak, the apostle explained: "A living God, a God of retribution, a jealous God, a God in need of nothing, consulting for the salvation of men, has sent me that I may reclaim them from corruption and uncleanness, and from all pleasure, and from death, that they may not sin." *A living God*, and hence unlike the idols fashioned by human hands. So also *a jealous God*, who will not share his adoration with others. *A God in need of nothing*, but rather one who generously shares his bounty. Then, too, a redemptive God, who commissioned Paul for service.

Having listened to the apostle's impassioned defense, the magistrate had him bound and incarcerated. He proposed to hear him further when not encumbered with more pressing duties. He may have been intent on receiving some remuneration in return for additional consideration.

Thecla bribed her way into prison, so that she could learn more from the apostle. "Sitting at his feet, she heard the great things of God. And Paul was afraid of nothing, but ordered his life in the confidence of God." In this regard, both served as exemplars, she as an earnest disciple and he as a fearless mentor.

When they found her, they brought Paul and Thecla before the tribunal. She was "exulting with joy." This recalls Jesus' encouragement: "Rejoice in that day (when reviled) and leap for joy, because great is your reward in heaven" (Luke 6:23).

The magistrate ordered that Paul be scourged and driven from the city. Moreover, he decreed that Thecla be burned. She searched the crowd to see if she could see the apostle. Instead, she saw the Lord in the similitude of Paul. As she gazed on him, he ascended into heaven.

"And she, having made the sign of the cross, went up on the fagots; and they lighted them." As observed earlier, the Christian martyr did not despise life, but cherished it by laying hold on eternal life.

"And though a great fire was blazing, it did not touch her; for God having compassion on her, made an underground rumbling, and a cloud overshadowed them from above, full of water and hail; and all that was in the cavity of it was poured out, so that many were in danger of death." Whereupon, the magistrate concluded that the gods meant that her life be spared.

"I have been saved from the fire," she concluded, "and am following Paul." When she found him, he was interceding on her behalf. She proposes to join him in the ministry, but he is reluctant—since she was beautiful and would likely be tempted to marry. "Now to the unmarried and the widows I say: It is good for them to stay unmarried, as I am," he earlier observed. "But if they cannot control themselves, they should marry, for it is better to marry than to burn with passion" (1 Cor. 7:8-9).

Paul subsequently relented, and Thecla accompanied him to Antioch. There she was accosted by a young man, who was much taken with her beauty. When she rejected him, he had her brought before the authorities. She was condemned to die, but "the lioness licked her feet." The multitude was astonished.

She was again brought into the arena, where there was an assortment of wild beasts. The lioness, having run to her, lay down at her feet. Then, when a bear attempted to approach, the lioness tore it to pieces. When other efforts were made to execute her, they failed as well. Meanwhile, a chorus of women (seemingly meant to personify justice) cried out against the proceedings. In this regard, the account resembles a stage production.

The magistrate finally issued an edict releasing Thecla. Whereupon, the chorus enthusiastically acclaimed: "There is one God, *the God* of Thecla."

She immediately went in search of the apostle. When she had come across him, he was astonished to see that she was accompanied by many others of like persuasion. It appears that her witness had borne a bountiful harvest.

In the course of time she announced her intent to press on to Iconium. "Go," Paul encouraged her, "and teach the word of God."

Upon returning to Iconium, she entered the house of Onesiphorus, and fell upon the place where Paul used to sit and teach her. She wept, saying: "God of myself and of this house, where You did make the light to shine upon me, O Christ Jesus, the Son of the living God, my help in the fire, my help among the wild beats, You are glorified for ever. Amen."

In this regard, "My soul will boast in the Lord; let the afflicted hear and rejoice. Glorify the Lord with me; let us exalt his name together" (Psa. 34:3-4). Moreover, "God is our refuge and strength, an ever-present help in trouble" (Psa. 46:1).

Thecla subsequently took leave for Rome, intent on meeting Paul there, but found that he had *fallen asleep*. She stayed on for some time, before she too reposed in a *glorious sleep*. She was buried two or three stadia (approximately 500 yards) from the tomb of the apostle.

Looking back over her life, she was cast into the fire when only seventeen years of age, and thrown to the beasts at eighteen. She lived in all seventy-two years. "And having accomplished many cures, she rests in the place of the saints, having fallen asleep on the twenty-fourth of the month of September in Christ Jesus our Lord, to whom be glory and strength for ever and ever." As a vibrant witness to the Lord's saving grace, and a beneficiary of Paul's zealous efforts. If fiction, as Tertullian alleges; then as a reminder that there is sometimes more truth in fiction that what passes as fact.

EXHORTATIONS

Paul's exhortations provide an additional insight into life in Christ. We shall focus our attention on the text of Romans, and more expressly that which begins with the twelfth chapter. The preceding deals with theological matters, while the remainder takes a more practical turn. Since the latter evolves from the former, it serves to get a running start.

The apostle had spent approximately a decade in church planting both east and west of the Aegean Sea. He now looked forward to expanding his ministry in other regions.

> A journey to Spain would afford him the opportunity of gratifying a long-standing ambition (to visit Rome). . . . All the more wonderful because there was a flourishing church in Rome, and several Christians whom Paul had met elsewhere in his travels were now resident in Rome and members of that church.[1]

Paul's letter to the Romans appears to have been his last correspondence prior to his prolonged incarceration. It seeks to establish rapport between the apostle and the congregation at Rome, which was likely established within two or three years after Jesus' passion. This should come as no surprise, since (as mentioned earlier) all roads were said to lead to Rome.

The apostle's line of thought can be briefly reconstructed. "I am not ashamed of the gospel, because it is the power of God for the salvation of everyone who believes," he declares at the outset. "For in the gospel a righteousness from God is revealed, a righteousness that is by faith from first to last" (1:16-17). First for the Jew, and then for the Gentile; in keeping with the pronouncement that the righteous shall live by faith.

In this connection, "all have sinned and fall short of the glory of God" (3:23). The religiously observant, as well as those who are not observant. Those acclaimed for their good works, as well as those who are inconsiderate of others. In proverbial terms, all are in the same boat.

Moreover, the boat is sinking. "For the wages of sin is death," Paul pointedly concludes, "but the gift of God is eternal life" (6:23). The exception *but* becomes normative in the course of salvation history.

This should not be used as an excuse for moral laxity. "Therefore do not let sin reign in your mortal body so that you obey its evil desires. . . . but rather offer yourselves to God, as those who have been brought from death to life" (6:12-13). No longer content to be under the dominion of sin, one seeks to cultivate God's sovereign and gracious will.

Paul subsequently expresses his sorrow that so many of his fellow Jews have failed to embrace the faith. "As God had his faithful remnant in earlier days, so he has in our day a remnant chosen by his grace. And as then, so now the remnant is a promise of better things to come; Israel's refusal of the gospel and consequent setting aside by God are only temporary."[2] One which allows for the ingathering of the Gentiles, and incites Israel to fortuitous jealously.

All things considered, we are encouraged to live out our faith in practice. In a way well-pleasing to God, edifying to self, commensurate with community, and as a witness to those outside the household of faith. In perpetuity, from one generation to the next—so long as the Lord should tarry.

Therefore (in the light of all that has been previously declared), "I urge you, brothers, in view of God's mercy, to offer your bodies as living sacrifices, holy and pleasing to God—this is your spiritual act of worship. Do not conform any longer to the pattern of this world, but be transformed by the renewing of your mind" (12:1-2).

Sacrifice is characterized in three ways: as living, holy, and pleasing to God. Since *living*, it solicits continuing attention. Since *holy*, it is not to be usurped for other purposes. Since *pleasing to God*, it requires that we put our priorities in order. This constitutes a *spiritual act of worship*, set over against perfunctory behavior.

The initial appeal is followed by a related one, contrasting two mutually exclusive alternatives. In negative terms, *do not be conformed any longer to the pattern of this world*. Where sin reigns unto death, and as a feeble echo of our cultural agenda. In positive terms, *be transformed by the renewing of your mind*. All things considered, embrace righteous change.

"Do not think of yourself more highly than your ought," the apostle continues to exhort his readers, "but rather think of yourself with sober judgment, in accordance with the measure of faith God has given you" (12:3). The admonition assumes that we may think of ourselves too highly. Conversely, others may give us less than our due. This calls for a more realistic appraisal.

"If a man's gift is prophesying, let him use it in proportion to his faith," Paul continues. "If it is serving, let him serve; if it is teaching, let him teach; if it is encouraging, let him encourage; if it is contributing, let him give generously; if it is leadership, let him govern diligently; if it is showing mercy, let him do it cheerfully." Let each person be diligent in his or her own calling, not exaggerating its importance or demeaning the contribution of others.

In proportion to his faith invokes the spiritual maturity of the individual. *Prophecy* heads the list of representative gifts. It consists of declaring God's word, characteristically concerning some pressing issue. On occasion, it involves some

Exhortations 81

future event—as an appeal to constructive action.

"Love must be sincere" introduces another series of exhortations (12:9). Love is often cited as the rationale for doing something that is self-seeking, and counter-productive. The apostle means to alert his readers to this temptation.

"Hate what is evil, cling to what is good." As for the former, we must distinguish between what the person does and the person as such. This is graphically conveyed by C. S. Lewis, who describes hell as the last place a loving God provides for those who will accept no better accommodation.

As for the latter, hold fast to all that is good. Do not let it escape your grasp, nor give up under duress. For it assuredly pays long-term interest, both in time and eternity.

"Be devoted to one another in brotherly love." "A friend loves at all times," the sage astutely reminds us, "and a brother is born of adversity" (Prov. 17:17). According to conventional wisdom, "Blood is thicker than water."

"Honor one another above yourselves." The apostle's reasoning seems obscure. He may be implying that since another person represents our service to Christ, then the individual is deserving of greater consideration.

"Never be lacking in zeal, but keep your spiritual fervor, serving the Lord." "Christians are constantly confronted by new challenges in life, in the face of which they cannot remain spectators. When such challenges represent the call of God and represent opportunities for serving Christ, idleness is disobedience."[3]

Instead, maintain a *spiritual fervor*. One that welcomes the dawn of each new day with the prospect of rendering some worthwhile service, remains alert throughout the day, and rests in confidence of the Lord's blessing.

"Be joyful in hope, patient in affliction, faithful in prayer." *Joyful in hope*, since all things work together for good to those who love God and are called according to his righteous purpose (cf. Rom. 8:28). *Patient in affliction*, as if an opportunity for refining one's faith. *Faithful in prayer*, because it provides a critical link in our relationship with the Almighty.

"Share with God's people who are in need." Not to the exclusion of those outside the fellowship, but with due deference to fellow believers. Then, not to be overlooked in the course of expanding our ministry in other ways.

"Practice hospitality," as if a special case in point. While an obligation, no less a privilege. Christians were to be exemplary in this connection.

Paul again shifts his approach, opting for a list of relatively unrelated topics. "Bless those who persecute you, bless and do not curse. Rejoice with those who rejoice; mourn with those who mourn. Live in harmony with one another. Do not be proud, but be willing to associate with people of low position. Do not be conceited" (12:15-16).

Bless those who persecute you, as a strategy for overcoming evil with good. Do not retaliate, but return good for evil. Persist in one's righteous resolve, obstacles notwithstanding.

Rejoice with those who rejoice; mourn with those who mourn. "There is a time for everything, and a season for every activity under heaven," the sage informs us.

In particular, "a time to weep and a time to laugh" (Eccles. 3:1, 4). We thus express our confidence that God is at work in all the vicissitudes of life for our eternal good. Consequently, we ought not to begrudge someone his or her cause for rejoicing, nor refrain from sharing the burden of another person's suffering.

Live in harmony with one another. Harmony implies a pleasing combination of elements. Each contributes something of worth in an appealing blend. In other words, constructive diversity.

Do not be proud, but willing to associate with people of low position. Do not be conceited. Pride fails to take into consideration how deeply we are indebted. To God most of all, since he is the source of life and its manifold blessings. To others in greater or lesser degree, because the sustaining of life takes a cooperative effort. Here it is expressly evidenced in an unwillingness to associate with persons of an inferior social cast.

Humility provides the preferred alternative. This does not imply self-flagellation, which might be construed as a negative expression of pride. It is rather a realistic appraisal of self, not given to excessive introspection.

The next series of exhortations is somewhat redundant.

> Do not repay anyone evil for evil. Be careful to do what is right in the eyes of everybody. If it is possible, as far as it depends on you, live at peace with everyone. Do not take revenge, but leave room for God's wrath . . . . Do not be overcome by evil, but overcome evil with good (12:17, 21).

The apostle again urges his readers not to retaliate, but let God set matters right.

What is right in the eyes of everybody is a reminder of conventional morality. Two things can be said in this regard. First, any culture provides a functional means through which to express the gospel. Consequently, we ought to resist the temptation of cultural colonialism.

Second, no culture is so pristine that it conforms to the high standards of Holy Writ. Some elements will deserve qualified commendation, while others must be modified, and still others rejected outright.

If it is possible

> implies that peace is not a compromise of good and cannot be purchased at any price. Christians must do all they can to promote peace and tolerance without betraying the will of God. When the good is at stake, however, believers have no alternative but to choose it, even at the risk of jeopardizing peace.[4]

Paul rounds off this series of exhortations with a general appeal not to be overcome by evil, but to overcome evil with good. As sometimes expressed, "All that is necessary for evil to triumph is for good people to do nothing."

"Everyone must submit himself to the governing authorities," the apostle insists, "for there is no authority except that which God has established. . . . For he is God's servant to do you good. But if you do wrong, be afraid, for he does not bear the sword for nothing" (13:1, 4). Since God is sovereign over all, the authorities are responsible to him for carrying out their duties.

Christians, conversely, are responsible to obey the authorities. Providing this does not violate the teaching of Scripture or the dictates of conscience. Even then, they must be prepared to bear the consequences of their action.

"This is why you pay taxes," the apostle observes. Since there are legitimate expenditures associated with governance. "If you owe taxes, pay taxes; if revenue, then revenue; if respect, then respect; if honor, then honor."

> The empire as a whole levied a property tax and a head tax; local provinces of kingdoms added further taxers; there were also customs duties. Taxes were used to finance roads and run the government but also to support Roman armies and temples devoted to the worship of the emperor.[5]

It goes without saying that the system was abused. This, coupled with the tax burden itself, solicited ill-feelings and the attempt to circumvent the code. It also carried over into a show of disrespect toward those in authority. Paul does not mean that his readers should ignore reality, but take a constructive approach.

"Let no debt remain outstanding, except the continuing debt to love one another, for he who loves his fellow man has fulfilled the law" (13:8). Be prompt in paying one's debts. In conventional terms, "Do not put off to tomorrow what you can do today."

The obligation to love one another proves to be the critical exception. In that it is not a debt that can ever be payed in full. We can, in a manner of speaking, make down-payments from time to time. As a reality check, love does not harm one's neighbor.

"The hour has come for you to wake up from your slumber, because our salvation is nearer now than when we first believed," the apostle continues.

> So let us put aside the deeds of darkness and put on the armor of light. Let us behave decently, as in the daytime, not in orgies and drunkenness, not in sexual immorality and debauchery, not in dissension and jealousy. Rather, clothe yourselves with the Lord Jesus Christ, and do not think about how to gratify the desires of the sinful nature (13:11-14).

We have been saved—at a given time in the past; *we are being saved*—as an ongoing process; and *we shall be saved*—as a consummate act.

Therefore, we ought to lay aside *the deeds of darkness and put on the armor of light*. As for the former, *orgies and drunkenness, sexual immorality and debauchery*, and *dissension and jealously*. In brief, a life of unbridled self-indulgence, without regard for the concerns of others.

As for the latter,

> in 'putting on Christ' believers discover that Christ's character and behavior become their own. This fare exceeds mere morality, important as that is. It means claiming Christ's identity as our identity, his way in the world as our way, and his promise of the future as our path in the present.[6]

Paul turns next to the need for reciprocal acceptance. "One man's faith allows him to eat everything, but another man, whose faith is weak, eats only vegetables," the apostle observes by way of illustration. "The man who eats everything must not look down on who does not, and the man who does not eat everything must not condemn the man who does, for God has accepted him" (14:2-3).

The apostle appears to be addressing a problem reported to him concerning the Roman fellowship. The *weak* are variously identified, as the following bears witness:

(1) The "weak" were mainly Gentile Christians who abstained from meat, particularly on certain 'fast' days, under the influence of certain pagan religions
(2) The "weak" were Christians, perhaps both Jewish and Gentile, who practiced an ascetic lifestyle for reasons we cannot determine.
(3) The "weak" were mainly Jewish Christians who observed certain practices derived from the Mosaic law out of concern to establish righteousness before God.
(4) The "weak" were mainly Jewish Christians who followed a sectarian program as a means of expressing their piety (perhaps in a syncretistic fashion).
(5) The "weak" were mainly Jewish Christians, who, like some of the Corinthians, believed that it was wrong to eat meat that was sold in (the) marketplace and was probably tainted by idolatry.
(6) The "weak" were mainly Jewish Christians who refrained from certain kinds of good and observed certain days out of continuing loyalty to the Mosaic law.[7]

Perhaps one of the above or in some combination. If the former, then most likely the last of the several options.

"Each one should be fully convinced in his own mind," the apostle adds. Which is to say that one should weigh the matter carefully, practice confidently, and be tolerant of those with whom he or she conscientiously disagrees. "But the man who has doubts is condemned if he eats, because . . . everything that does not come from faith is sin."

"Accept one another, then, just as Christ accepted you, in order to bring glory to God" (15:7). Out of compassion, without thought of self, that others may be built up in the faith. So also as a matter of pious resolve, out of devotion to the Almighty, that his name be glorified. In this regard, "May the God who gives endurance and encouragement give you a spirit of unity among yourselves as you follow Christ Jesus."

The letter now takes a decidedly personal turn. "I myself am convinced, my brothers, that you yourselves are full of goodness, complete in knowledge and competent to instruct one another" (15:14). He, nonetheless, does not hesitate to assume his prerogative as the apostle to the Gentiles, and so present them as an "offering acceptable to God, sanctified by the Holy Spirit."

"It has always been my ambition to preach the gospel where Christ was not known," the apostle confides, "so that I would not be building on someone else's foundation" (15:20). "Paul indicates that he believed that God had given him the ministry of establishing strategic churches in virgin gospel territory; like the early Christian pioneers who pulled up stakes anytime they could see the smoke from another person's cabin."[8]

"I urge you, brothers, by our Lord Jesus Christ and by the love of the Spirit, to join me in my struggle by praying to God for me," the apostle again enjoins them. "Pray that I may be rescued from the unbelievers in Judea and that my service in Jerusalem may be acceptable to the saints there, so that by God's will I may come to you with joy and together with you be refreshed" (15:30-32).

The allusion to *my struggle* vividly reflects Paul's frame of mind. He faced a serious threat in returning to Jerusalem. He was also uncertain as to his reception by fellow believers, given his much maligned ministry. It is not surprising that he implores those in Rome to bear him up in prayer, and thus share his burden.

"I commend to you our sister Phoebe, as servant of the church in Cenchrea," Paul entreats them. "I ask you to receive her in the Lord in a way worthy of the saints and to give her any help she may need from you, for she has been a great help to many people, including me" (16:1-2). She appears be a person of considerable means, influence, or both; and may have been the bearer of his correspondence.

Paul now admonishes the recipients of his epistle to extend his greeting to various persons. About a third of the names mentioned are women, suggesting the critical role they played in the fellowship. "Greet Priscilla and Aquila, my fellow workers in Christ Jesus. They risked their lives for me. Not only I but all the churches of the Gentiles are grateful to them."

"Greet also the church that meets at their house." The house churches provided a considerable impetus to the spread of the gospel. Such meeting places might accommodate extended family, business associates, and slaves.

"Greet my dear friend Epenetus, who was the first convert of Christ in the province of Asia." We know only that he took the first bold step of faith.

"Greet Mary, who worked very hard for you." She was apparently a Jewess, whose labors are appreciatively recalled.

"Greet Andronicus and Junia, my relatives who have been in prison with me. They are outstanding among the apostles, and they were in Christ before I was." *My relatives* appears to be a reference to their Jewish identity. They were *apostles* in a more general sense than applied to the Twelve.

Later on, "Greet Apelles, tested and approved in Christ." While the name appears among the royal household, he was in any case one whose faith was refined in adversity.

"Greet those in the household of Aristobulus." This might be a reference to the grandson of Herod I and brother of Agrippa I, who lived in Rome and was a friend of Emperor Claudius. The latter was perhaps deceased or not a convert.

"Greet Herodion, my relative." Given the name and its location, he was probably also related to the above family.

Still later on, "Greet Typhina and Typhosa, those women who work hard in the Lord. Greet my dear friend Persis, another woman who has worked very hard in the Lord." All three are Greek names, and the first two may have been sisters. All are characterized by their diligent labors.

"Greet Rufus, chosen in the Lord, and his mother who has been a mother to me, too." *Rufus* was a common slave name, his mother was applauded for taking a maternal concern for others.

Then, finally, the apostle admonished: "Greet one another with a holy kiss." It was a form of social respect, adopted as a means of expressing a common bond in Christ. He then urges them to beware of those who would create divisions, and thereby disregard the teaching they had received.

In these and other ways, living a life consistent with being in Christ. Thereby heeding the admonition of the apostle, by putting faith into practice. Then, in turn, experiencing the Lord's lavish blessing.

ENDNOTES

Preface

1. Paul Barnett, *The Second Epistle to the Corinthians*, p. 298.

Chapter 1: Correspondence

1. R. Alan Cole, *Galatians*, p. 25.
2. Oscar Brooks, *The Drama of Decision*, p. 31.
3. David Williams, *1 and 2 Thessalonians*, p. 99.
4. Donald Guthrie, *New Testament Theology*, p. 667.
5. Colin Kruse, *2 Corinthians*, p. 85.
6. James Edwards, *Romans*, p. 175.
7. Ibid., p. 286.
8. Arthur Patzia, *Ephesians, Colossians, Philemon*, p. 7.
9. F. F. Bruce, *The Epistle to the Colossians, to Philemon, and to the Ephesians*, p. 253.
10. Guthrie, *op. cit.*, p. 594.
11. F. F. Bruce, *Philippians*, p. 113.
12. Patzia, *op. cit.*, p. 109.
13. Donald Guthrie, *The Pastoral Epistles*, p. 17.

Chapter 2: Jesus of History

1. Morris Inch, *Two Gospel Motifs*, pp. 3-100.
2. Leon Morris, *Luke*, p. 96.
3. *The Gospel of Infancy*, 13, 2-3.
4. Morris, *op. cit.*, p. 132.
5. Guthrie, *op. cit.*, pp. 412-413.

6. Yechiel Eckstein, *How Firm a Foundation*, p. 94.
7. Morris, *op. cit.*, p. 197.
8. Marvin Wilson, *Our Father Abraham*, pp. 246-247.
9. Inch, *op. cit.*, p. 79.

Chapter 3: Christ of Faith

1. Rudolf Bultmann, *Jesus and the Word*, p. vi.
2. F. F. Bruce, *Paul: Apostle of the Heart Set Free*, pp. 69-70.
3. David Williams, *Acts*, p. 169.
4. I. Howard Marshall, *Acts*, p. 261.
5. Craig Keener, *The IVP Bible Background Commentary: New Testament*, p. 514.

Chapter 4: One Among Many

1. Eckstein, *op. cit.*, p. 63.
2. Ibid., p. 84.
3. Ibid., p. 94.
4. Gordon Wenham *Genesis 1-15*, p. 71.
5. Moises Silva, *Philippians*, p. 177.
6. David Aune, "Human Nature and Ethics in Hellenistic Philosophic Tradition and Paul," *Paul in His Hellenistic Context* (Engberg-Pedersen, ed), p. 291.
7. Josephus, *The Antiquities of the Jews*, 18. 1. 3.
8. Edwards, *op. cit.*, p. 194.
9. Keener, *op. cit.*, p. 375.
10. *Acts of Paul and Thecla*.

Chapter 5: A Corporate Identity

1. Raphael Patai, *Society, Culture, and Change in the Middle East*, p. 267.
2. Ibid., p. 276.
3. Walter Brueggemann, *Living Toward a Vision*, p. 28.
4. Ibid., p. 30.
5. Dietrich Bonhoeffer, *Ethics*, p. 207.
6. Ibid., p. 210.
7. Gordon Fee, *The First Epistle to the Corinthians*, p. 603.
8. Helmut Thielicke, *I Believe*, p. 237.

Chapter 6: In Situ

1. John Bimson (ed.), *Baker Encyclopedia of Bible Places*, p. 295.
2. F. F. Bruce, *The Book of the Acts*, p. 163.
3. Bimson, *op. cit.*, p. 26.

4. Williams, *Acts*, p. 224.
5. Bruce, *The Book of Acts*, p. 329.

Chapter 7: Salvation History

1. Morris Inch, *Scripture As Story*, p. 9.
2. John Milton, *Paradise Lost*, XII, 36-45.
3. R. Alan Cole, *Exodus*, p. 56.
4. Herbert Wolf, *An Introduction to the Old Testament Pentateuch*, p. 132.
5. Inch, *Scripture As Story*, p. 35.

Chapter 8: The Angels' View

1. Francis Foulkes, *Ephesians*, p. 54.
2. John Polkinghorne, *Quarks, Chaos & Christianity*, p. 91.
3. Guthrie, *New Testament Theology*, pp. 319-320.
4. F. F. Bruce, *The Epistle to the Hebrews*, pp. 116-117.
5. Thielicke, *op. cit.*, p. 197.
6. Harry Boer, *A Short History of the Christian Church*, p. 53.

Chapter 9: Paul As Paradigm

1. Fee, *op. cit.*, p. 186.
2. Tertullian, *Against Marcion*, xxi.
3. Tertullian, *Against Praxeas*, xxviii.
4. *The Treatise of Athenagorous*, iii.
5. Irenaeus, *Against Heresies*, III. xv, 1.
6. Bruce, *Paul: Apostle of the Heart Set Free*, p. 18.
7. Irenaeus, *op. cit.*, II. xxx. 7.
8. Origin, *De Principiis*, III. 7.
9. *Elucidations*, I.
10. Irenaeus, *op. oit.*, III. vii. 2.
11. Tertullian, *Against Marcion*, xx.
12. Tertullian, *Scorplace*, xiii.
13. *Acts of Paul and Thecla*.

Chapter 10: Exhortations

1. F. F. Bruce, *Romans*, p. 14.
2. Ibid., p. 62.
3. Edwards, *op. cit.*, p. 293.
4. Ibid., p. 298.
5. Keener, *op. cit.*, p. 441.

6. Edwards, *op. cit.*, p. 316.
7. Douglas Moo, *The Epistle to the Romans*, pp. 828-829.
8. Ibid., p. 396.

BIBLIOGRAPHY

Acts of Paul and Thecla. Alexander and Donaldson (eds.). *Ante-Nicene Fathers.* vol. 2, 487-492.
Alexander, Roberts and James Donaldson (eds.). *Ante-Nicene Fathers.* Peabody: Hendrickson, 1994.
Aune, David. "Human Nature and Ethics in Hellenistic Philosophical Traditions and Paul," *Paul in His Hellenistic Context* (Engberg-Pedersen, ed.), 291-312.
Barnett, Paul. *The Second Epistle to the Corinthians.* Grand Rapids: Eerdmans, 1997.
Bimson, John. *Baker Encyclopedia of Bible Places.* Grand Rapids: Baker, 1995.
Boer, Harry. *A Short History of the Christian Church.* Grand Rapids: Eerdmans, 1978.
Bonhoeffer, Dietrich. *Ethics.* New York: Macmillan, 1963.
Brooks, Oscar. *The Drama of Decision: Baptism in the New Testament.* Peabody: Hendrickson, 1993.
F. F. Bruce. *The Book of Acts.* Grand Rapids: Eerdmans, 1988.
———. *The Epistle to the Hebrews.* Grand Rapids: Eerdmans, 1990.
———. *The Epistle to the Colossians, to Philemon and to the Ephesians.* Grand Rapids: Eerdmans, 1984.
———. *Paul: Apostle of the Heart Set Free.* Grand Rapids: Eerdmans, 1999.
———. *Philippians.* Peabody: Hendrickson, 1993.
———. *Romans.* Downers Grove: Inter-Varsity, 1992.
Brueggemann, Walter. *Living Toward a Vision.* Philadelphia: United Church, 1976.
Bultmann, Rudolf. *Jesus and the Word.* New York: Scribner's, 1958.
Cole, R. Alan. *Exodus.* Downers Grove: Inter-Varsity, 1973.
———. *Galatians.* Downers Grove: Inter-Varsity, 1991.
Eckstein, Yechiel. *How Firm a Foundation.* Brewster: Paraclete, 1997.
Edwards, James. *Romans.* Peabody: Hendrickson, 1993.
Elucidations. Alexander and Donaldson (eds). *Ante-Nicene Fathers.* vol. 4, 282-284.
Engberg-Pedersen (ed.). *Paul in His Hellenistic Context.* Minneapolis: Fortress, 1995.
Fee, Gordon. *The First Epistle to the Corinthians.* Grand Rapids: Eerdmans, 1987.
Foulkes, Francis. *Ephesians.* Downers Grove: Inter-Varsity, 1989.
The Gospel of Infancy. Alexander and Donaldson (eds). *Ante-Nicene Fathers.* vol. 8, 405-415.

Guthrie, Donald. *New Testament Theology*. Downers Grove: Inter-Varsity, 1981.
———. *The Pastoral Epistles*. Grand Rapids: Eerdmans, 1992.
Inch, Morris. *Scripture As Story*. Lanham: University Press of America, 2000.
———. *Two Gospel Motifs: The Original Quest & The Messianic Theophany*. Lanham: University Press of America, 2001.
Irenaeus. *Against Heresies*. Alexander and Donaldson (eds.) *Ante-Nicene Fathers*. vol. 1, 315-367.
Josephus. *The Antiquities of the Jews*. Peabody: Hendrickson, 2000.
Kearns, George, et. al. *English and Western Literature*. New York: Macmillan, 1987.
Keener, Craig. *The IVP Bible Background Commentary: New Testament*. Downers Grove: Inter-Varsity, 1993.
Kruse, Colin. *2 Corinthians*. Downers Grove: Inter-Varsity, 1991.
Marshall, I. Howard. *Acts*. Downers Grove: Inter-Varsity, 1991.
Milton, John. *Paradise Lost*. Kearns (ed.) *English and Western Literature*. 230-235.
Moo, Douglass. *The Epistle to the Romans*. Grand Rapids: Eerdmans, 1996.
Morris, Leon. *Luke*. Downers Grove: Inter-Varsity, 1990.
Origin. *De Principii*. Roberts and Donaldson (ed.). *Ante-Nicene Fathers*. vol. 4, 239-382.
Patai, Raphael. *Society, Culture, and Change in the Middle East*. Philadelphia: University of Pennsylvania, 1971.
Patzia, Arthur. *Ephesians, Colossians, Philemon*. Peabody: Hendrickson, 1993.
Polkinghorne, John. *Quarks, Chaos & Christianity*. New York: Crossroad, 1994.
Silva, Moises. *Philippians*. Grand Rapids: Baker, 1992.
Tertullian. *Against Marion*. Alexander and Donaldson (eds.). *Ante-Nicene Fathers*. vol. 3, 271-474.
———. *Against Praxes*. Alexander and Donaldson (eds.). *Ante-Nicene Fathers*. vol. 3, 597-627.
———. *Scorplace*. Alexander and Donaldson (eds.). *Ante-Nicene Fathers*. vol. 3, 633-648.
Thielicke, Helmut. *I Believe: The Christian's Creed*. Philadelphia: Fortress, 1986.
The Treatise of Athenagorous. Alexander and Donaldson (eds.). *Ante-Nicene Fathers*. vol. 2, 149-162.
Wenham, Gordon. *Genesis 1-15*. Dallas: Word, 1991.
Williams, David. *1 and 2 Thessalonians*. Peabody: Hendrickson, 1994.
Wilson, Marvin. *Our Father Abraham: Jewish Roots of the Christian Faith*. Grand Rapids: Eerdmans, 1989.
Wolf, Herbert. *An Introduction to the Old Testament Pentateuch*. Chicago: Moody, 1991.

INDEX

apostolic calling, 5, 16.5, 36, 70-71
ascension, v, 3-5, 23, 63-68

baptism, 1, 15

Christ of faith, v, 13, 25-30
church, 35, 43-45
community, 7, 10, 39-45, 79-81
correspondence, 1-11
    early epistles, 1-3
    major epistles, 3-6
    prison epistles, 7-9
    pastoral epistles, 10-11

cost of discipleship, 16, 22, 78, 83

faith, 1, 4-7, 9-10, 36-37, 50, 57, 68, 70, 77, 81
love, 2, 4, 6-10, 17-18, 36, 64, 79, 81-82

marriage and family, 14-15, 34, 39-40, 42-43, 83
Messiah, 15, 17, 22, 32, 55, 67
Moses, 5, 16-17, 57-58

Passover, 20-21, 32
Paul as paradigm, 31-37, 69-76, 82
Pentecost, 32, 66-67

glory of God, 2, 5, 8, 14, 77, 82
gospel, 1, 7-8, 17, 45, 81-82
grace, 2-6, 8, 11, 14, 27-30, 48, 71, 77

Holy Spirit, 15, 23, 27-28, 44, 49, 53, 61, 65-68, 72, 81-82
hope, 7-8, 63, 79

Jerusalem Council, 1, 50
Jesus of history, v, 3, 13-23, 25-26, 60
    early years, 13-15
    public ministry, 15-16, 61
    Jerusalem bound, 18-19
    passion narrative, 20-23, 61
justification, 1-3, 5, 8

Kingdom of God, 17-18, 25, 45, 80

prayer, 3, 5, 7, 17, 20-21, 49, 79

redemption, 5-6, 8, 14, 33, 74
repentance, 8, 15, 19, 68, 70
resurrection, 2-3, 22, 26, 48, 68, 7-71

salvation, 5, 8, 11, 81
salvation history, v, 55-61
sanctification, 3, 10-11, 37, 66, 78
spiritual, 4-5, 7, 11, 78-79

Thecla, 74-76
Torah (teaching, law), 1-2, 5-6, 18, 26, 34-35, 57

wisdom, 4, 7, 14, 29

www.ingramcontent.com/pod-product-compliance
Lightning Source LLC
Chambersburg PA
CBHW021133300426
44113CB00006B/411